C

NORTHERNIZING THE SOUTH

NORTHERNIZING

THE SOUTH

RICHARD N. CURRENT

MERCER UNIVERSITY
LAMAR MEMORIAL LECTURES
No. 26

THE UNIVERSITY OF GEORGIA PRESS

ATHENS

Set in 11 on 13 pt. Linotron 202 Baskerville
Printed in the United States of America

The paper in this book meets the guidelines for
permanence and durability of the Committee on
Production Guidelines for Book Longevity of the
Council on Library Resources.

Library of Congress Cataloging in Publication Data

Current, Richard Nelson.
Northernizing the South.

(Lamar memorial lectures; no. 26)
Bibliography: p.
Includes index.
1. Southern States—Civilization—Addresses, essays,
lectures. 2. Regionalism—Southern States—
Addresses, essays, lectures. I. Title. II. Series.
F209.5.C87   1983   974'.03   82–23804
ISBN 0–8203–0666–5

*To my students
during twenty-three years
in Maryland, New Jersey, New York, Michigan,
Wisconsin, California, and Illinois,
and twenty-two years in North Carolina.*

Contents

Foreword

AT THE VERY BEGINNING OF THE AMERICAN NATION, MOST of the Founding Fathers from the South not only believed that their region was distinctive but that its interests were threatened by the rest of the country. Over the first half of the nineteenth century, as crises developed over the expansion of slavery and over states' rights, Southern fears of being Northernized grew. Determined to resist further demands to conform to Northern standards, Southern states by 1860 began to leave the Union and very soon thereafter to fight.

The intensity and the lengthiness of the Civil War strengthened rather than diminished the North's resolve to transform the South. That resolve, seemingly indomitably maintained in Congressional Reconstruction, in turn spurred the South to oppose efforts to Northernize it all the more. So staunch was Southern recalcitrance that by the end of the 1870s the North abandoned its attempt to regenerate its old enemy.

Still, Southerners perceived threats, even though for the next seventy-five years Northerners seldom tried to remake the South in the image of their section. After the Second World War, however, such fundamental change occurred—sometimes urged by Northerners, sometimes by Southerners themselves—that similarities between the sections were far more significant than differences. The land below the Potomac was passing from the age of New South to that of "No South." Hardly anywhere except in the imagination of self-conscious Southerners did Southern distinctiveness linger.

Such, in summary, is Richard N. Current's argument in the pages that follow. If there is anything certain in Southern studies it is that cultivators of that field agree to disagree over whether the South continues to possess a distinctive culture. At virtually the same time that Professor Current advanced his interpretation in the course of delivering the twenty-sixth Lamar Memorial Lectures at Mercer University in October 1982, historians participating in a symposium at Duke University argued for the persistence of Southern distinctiveness.

To foster informed discussion of Southern culture was a goal of Mrs. Eugenia Dorothy Blount Lamar when, through a bequest, she established this lecture series named in her honor. We at Mercer welcome Professor Current's timely, provocative contribution to that ongoing discussion.

Wayne Mixon
for the
Lamar Memorial Lectures Committee

Preface

I WISH, FIRST, TO THANK MERCER UNIVERSITY AND, more particularly, the members of the Lamar Memorial Lectures committee for inviting me to deliver the lectures for 1982. To be chosen as one of the participants in this distinguished series is a high honor indeed, and I am grateful for it.

I wish, second, to thank the university community and the lectures committee for the reception they gave Mrs. Current and me during our visit, a reception as kind and friendly as the sunny October weather. We are especially indebted to Patricia and Henry Warnock for their hospitality. Touring antebellum mansions with Professor Warnock, we were delighted to discover not only that Sherman had spared Macon (except for the one cannon ball) but also that in the intervening years the city has not been utterly Northernized.

I wish, finally, to thank Charles East, Karen Orchard, and Ann Lowry Weir—assistant director, managing editor, and freelance copyeditor of the University of Georgia Press—for their excellent work in preparing the manuscript for publication. To join the list of University of Georgia Press authors is an added honor.

R. N. C.

Introduction

THESE LECTURES UNDERTAKE TO TRACE, FROM THE 1780s
to the 1980s, the hopes of Northerners and the fears of
Southerners that someday the South would be, in character and culture, identical with the North. The topic is,
of course, closely related to the broader and more familiar one of Southern character and culture itself, which
has engaged countless authors, some of whom have
touched upon the Northernizing aspect, but none of
whom has attempted to treat it at any length. The sub-
stance is not one of "facts" in the usual sense, but one of
desires, impressions, and beliefs. In preparing the lectures I have read, among other things, a number of ac-
counts that came from Northerners traveling or residing
in the South. Since I am a Northerner residing in the
South, or a Southerner coming from the North, I might
introduce the topic and myself by summarizing my own
impressions of the South and its changing ways.

I was a twenty-four-year-old graduate student at the
University of Wisconsin when I first set foot on Southern
soil. Having been born and raised in Colorado, and having studied in Ohio and Massachusetts, I thought I knew
pretty well the country from the Rocky Mountains to the
rock-bound coast of Maine. But the South was *terra in-
cognita* to me until, in the summer of 1937, I toured

every former Confederate state east of the Mississippi River.

Some of my memories of that trip remain vivid after the lapse of forty-five years. On the whole I felt at least as much like a foreigner as I was to feel when, years later, I first went abroad. Much of the landscape was strange, especially in moonlit woods where the Spanish moss wrought its eerie effect. The language, though more or less intelligible, was certainly not the same as mine. This language difference struck me one night when, lost on a detour between Vicksburg and Natchez, I stopped at a crossroads store to ask directions. After getting them, I prolonged my conversation with the fat, smiling, sweating grocer-woman just to listen to her broad Mississippi accent, and she seemed equally willing to converse as she sat in her rocking chair and fanned herself. Finally she stopped rocking and fanning and said: "You know, I've got a cousin in Chicago talks exactly like you!" I suddenly realized what had never occurred to me before: that I, too, had an accent, and that there were people who considered it something of a curiosity. After that I came to believe, and I still believe, that, of all the real or imagined differences between Northerners and Southerners, the speech difference is not only the most noticeable but also the most fundamental. In reading about variations in regional character, I have found it hard to understand why authors—Northern, Southern, and foreign—so seldom mention this point and make so little of it when they do.

During that depression decade of the 1930s things were shabby enough in the Northern states in which I had lived or traveled, but far shabbier in the South. Here false-fronted, wooden corner stores still persisted in large numbers. They usually needed paint, and they often sold candy bars that were stale, discolored and misshapen from the summer heat, or crawling with worms. In the field the farmer with a battered straw hat, and sometimes with bare feet, trudged behind the mule-drawn plow. Tractors were seldom seen. At the filling station black men put gasoline in the tank, checked the oil, and washed the windshield, while white men sat in chairs tilted against the wall on the shady side of the building, one of these men waiting for the motorist to bring him the money. The campgrounds and tourist cabins (in that pre-motel age) were mostly unkempt and primitive. At one such place the proprietress complained quite frankly to prospective customers that she simply could not keep up with the bedbugs. Shabbiness, backwardness, shift-lessness, slovenliness—such traits then seemed to me fairly characteristic of Southerners and the South.

Also striking, to someone new to the region, was the presence of so many blacks. Even more striking was the way in which they and the whites lived together and yet apart. My first impressions of Southern race relations were confirmed in the course of the four years, 1938–1942, that I spent on the Eastern Shore of Maryland. You might not consider these as four years spent in the South. Some people would not include them at all. There is a Lincoln story about a witness who kept insisting that his age was sixty, though he looked much older. When the judge finally intervened to ask him if he had not perhaps overlooked a part of his life, the old man brightened up and said: "Oh, you must be thinking of the ten years I spent on the Eastern Shore of Maryland. I don't count them." I do count my four years there, and I treasure them, but I am glad that times have changed there, as elsewhere.

When I arrived in Salisbury, on the Eastern Shore, the inhabitants, white and black, could remember all too well a recent and particularly horrible lynching. Blacks, in slums that few whites ever saw, lived in weather-beaten shacks that rested on corner piers and were vulnerable to the winter wind, even on the underside. The houses had no plumbing, and water had to be brought from community faucets at the intersections of streets which were not paved. Outside these ghettoes there was no place where whites could meet socially with blacks. Segregation was strictest on the Eastern Shore, but it was also *de rigueur* in other parts of the state. In Baltimore the University of Maryland hospital, a skyscraper containing the most modern equipment, had two widely separated street entrances, alike except that over one was engraved in stone the word "white," and over the other the word "colored."

Conditions had changed little when I returned to the South after thirteen migratory years in New Jersey, New York, Michigan, Wisconsin, California, and Illinois. The Supreme Court had yet to announce its decision in *Brown* v. *Board of Education* when, in March 1954, I made a preliminary trip from Champaign, Illinois, to Greensboro, North Carolina. Changing trains in Washington, D.C., I started to board a coach when a black trainman took me by the arm and wordlessly led me to another coach, one that looked the same but was set aside for whites rather than blacks. At the then very busy Greensboro station, the black waiting room was not even visible from the white one. In the station and also in the downtown stores there were dual drinking fountains and dual sets of restrooms, with their "white" and "colored" signs. At the Woman's College of the University of North Carolina the only blacks were janitors or maids.

As I got to know North Carolinians, I soon concluded that, if those I met were representative, then Southerners were indeed different from Northerners, at least in certain respects. Southerners showed an incomparable concern with kinship: they wanted to be sure they got straight everyone's family background and connections. Southerners were unbelievably hospitable, unbelievably generous with invitations. They were extremely polite, careful to say "No, ma'm," or "Yes, sir." And they were remarkably considerate, eager to yield to those ahead of them in a line. A newcomer from the North, used to pushing and shoving to maintain his position, might almost fall on his face as the Southerners quickly and courteously stepped aside.

But the longer I lived in the South, the less real and the less important the differences seemed to be. Southern hospitality, the newcomer learned in due course, was unbelievable indeed. It was largely verbal. A newcomer risked embarrassment if, when a recent acquaintance urged him to "Come on over, y'hear," he took the invitation seriously and responded: "Thanks very much. When would be a good time?" Sooner or later the Northerner also discovered that Southern politeness was pretty much a formality. The well-bred child could utter his "No, ma'm" or "Yes, sir" in a surly tone that made the expression much less polite than an honest and straightforward "Yes" or "No." As for Southern courtesy or considerateness, this too proved to have definite limits. It was operative in face-to-face situations but not in impersonal or anonymous ones. Thus, in Greensboro, the patrons of McDonald's typically left the parking area strewn with trash; in Madison, Wisconsin, they left it comparatively tidy and neat. Still, the conviction grew upon me that, on the whole, Northerners and Southerners were about equal in virtue and vice, and that their vices and virtues were essentially the same.

In time, with economic and social progress, the South (or at least the part of it that I was most familiar with) overtook and even passed the North (or many parts of it) in qualities that Northerners liked to think of as distinctively Northern. Expanding industries, cities, suburbs, shopping centers, throughways—these made business enterprise and a passion for modernity seem like veritable Southern traits. In population and production, Greensboro surpassed Utica, New York, near which I had formerly lived, and which once had been much larger and more up to date. By the 1970s, Greensboro and a number of other Southern cities had peacefully integrated their schools. Many Northern cities—including Pontiac, Denver, and Boston—were scenes of violent resistance; some, such as Chicago, had not even attempted desegregation. Thus, in many instances, the South was more willing than the North to comply with federal law.

This contrast revealed for all to see the hypocrisy and bigotry that Northerners all along had harbored with respect to the South. When I was about to leave Illinois for North Carolina in 1955, a colleague asked how I could live in a place where they treated blacks as they did down there. In Champaign at that time the grade schools were completely segregated *de facto*, the black slums were at least as miserable as the worst in Greensboro, and the university's star football player, being black, could not get a haircut in any of the area's barbershops. When, in the 1960s, an Alabama mob fell upon a busload of "freedom riders" and one of them turned out to be from Appleton, Wisconsin, I was reminded of my arrival in that town in 1945. An Appleton merchant greeted me: "You're new in town? Well, I want you to know Appleton is a fine place. Yes, sir. We don't allow no niggers here. We say: 'Nigger, don't let the sun set on you in Appleton.'" As I recalled that incident, I could not help thinking that the Appleton freedom rider need not have gone all the way to Alabama: he could have done his freedom-riding on a local bus.

The supercilious attitude of Northerners is seen in much of the news magazine and television commentary on recent events in the South, such as the Joanne Little case, the federal government's "desegregation" proceedings against the University of North Carolina, and the Greensboro shoot-out between the Communist Workers and the Ku Klux Klan. The same supercilious attitude finds private expression in the remarks of some Northerners living in the South. I am thinking, for example, of the woman from Indiana who once told me—in the most nasal, harsh, and whiny Hoosier accent—how disagreeable she considered Southern speech.

My defensiveness in response to Northern criticisms of the South was perhaps a measure of my assimilation as a Southerner or, at any rate, as a North Carolinian. Earlier I had felt self-conscious in the presence of native Tar Heels, such as the elderly farm woman who once asked me where I was from. When I said I was from Greensboro, she was not satisfied, and I had to confess that I was really from up North. "I thought so," she remarked. "I could tell by your brogue." (In most of the English-speaking world a "brogue" is an Irish accent; in the American South it is a Northern accent.) Eventually, more than a quarter-century after first moving to Greensboro (I had moved to Greensboro a second time, following another stint, this one of about five years, in Wisconsin), I had practically lost that feeling of foreignness. I did not know whether this was because Greensboro had changed so much—or because I had.

Then I was made to realize that anti-Yankee feeling was not entirely a thing of the past, even in Greensboro. The revelation came from the articles of a local columnist in the *Greensboro Daily News* on August 21, 31, September

4 and 11, 1981. The columnist, Jerry Bledsoe, began
with a casual reference to an event he had witnessed on
a North Carolina beach: "Some Yankee tourists were
torturing a ghost crab." When one of his readers, originally a New Yorker, raised the question whether the
"Yankee tourists" might not have been native North Carolinians, Bledsoe replied, quite irrelevantly:

> I could try to squirm out of this and say I used Yankee merely as
> a descriptive term and intended no derogatory meaning. I won't do
> that. For many native Southerners, prejudice against Northerners is
> more deeply ingrained than prejudice against blacks ever was (al-
> though not as deep as Northerners' prejudice against Southerners).
> Many Southerners who completely overcame prejudice against blacks
> still harbor dark thoughts about Yankees.
>
> Despite my best intentions, I haven't quite been able to conquer
> this in myself. Every time I see somebody from New Jersey doing
> something atrocious, especially in North Carolina, this prejudice
> bubbles up. I need only see somebody with a northern accent being
> pushy, strident and generally uncivilized to have the Yankee stereo-
> type reinforced. I know, of course, that many Northerners don't fit
> this stereotype, and I wrestle regularly with this bigotry, but every
> time I think I've got it pinned, it jumps back up again.

These remarks aroused so much interest that Bledsoe
devoted another column to the "Yankee problem." He
asserted that Yankees had "so fouled Yankeeland that it
is no longer habitable," and therefore they were fleeing
southward. "The trouble with so many of these immigrants is that they tend to remain Yankees after they get
here," Bledsoe explained. "They look down their noses
at local fashions and customs and have no desire to be
assimilated. Instead, they want to remake North Carolina into New Jersey or Ohio or whatever." Bledsoe went
on to propose measures "to protect what is left of our
unique culture." These measures included "immigration
quotas for Yankees," the requirement of "an affidavit
agreeing to the nobility of grits" and of other Southern-

isms, and "assimilation schools" that would teach new-comers such "essential things" as "how to talk right."

Bledsoe had begun to seek refuge behind a pretense of humor. A week later he complained of the abuse he had received merely because of a "joshing little column" he had written. "Talk about not being able to take a joke—a lot of these newly arrived Yankees quickly presented classic examples. And kept at it all week." Bledsoe said it would be "easy to dismiss the nasty response" as "typically Yankee" if a "charming person" from New Jersey had not demonstrated that at least one Northerner was different. This woman brought him a reply in the form of verse, which included the following:

> We love the sounds of Southern speech.
> Your heroes we revere.
> If any other were the case,
> We'd surely not be here.
>
> We've learned to say "Y'all come back!"
> Instead of "Hey, You Guys!"
> As for assimilating, friend,
> We Yankees take the prize.

Among the letters that the columnist inspired and the newspaper printed was one from another woman who also was eager to be assimilated and accepted. "Why, I hardly consider myself a Yankee, having been born and reared in Ohio," she wrote. "I am one of those who has moved and subsequently fallen in love with the South and stayed." She and her family suffered "dietary shock at first," but "now the cooking comes naturally and the family begs for cornbread, hominy, ham biscuits, great greens, and grits." She guessed "it's every 'damned Yan-kee's' dream to possess a bit of the history of the South for himself." She apologized: "It was a mere accident of birth that we started out in the North. Please—don't hold it against us."

If any born-and-bred Southerner sympathized with
these would-be Southerners from the North, or was inclined to rebuke the columnist for his anti-Yankee dia-
tribes, no letter from such a person appeared in the
newspaper. But letters did appear from natives who endorsed the Bledsoe program. "His feelings toward the
Yankee invasion are felt by quite a few southerners in
Guilford County," one attested, then added a request for
the publication of "additional articles which may help
some of the northerners be aware of their faults and try
to help the South continue to be the best place to live."
Another correspondent offered to assist in developing
the curriculum for a "Yankee Assimilation Academy"
and said he was preparing "a 100-item multiple-choice
placement test including questions about cornpone,
cracklin' bread, soup beans, possums, fox hunts, hominy, magnolias," and so forth.

Though some of these discussants were attempting a
light and humorous touch, they were undoubtedly making a judgment as well as a jest. But several of the
Northern-born saw nothing funny in the discussion. One
thought Bledsoe had a "rednecked" and "ignorant" point
of view. "Bledsoe should be reminded that North Carolina and our area specifically is actively trying to attract
northern industry so that the general population can
find employment other than spitting and tuning up old
cars," another wrote. "Much like missionaries in the midst
of savages, we try to show by example that there is more
to life than flea markets." A "Midwest Yankee" declared:
"I love your South! We've been here six years and we
will always remain Yankees. Like I tell my Yankee children, 'the South will rise again—with the Yankee's help!'"
Another Northerner swore he would not go back North
for love or money, but he also avowed: "I believe the
Yankees who won the war over a hundred years ago gave

the South a hundred years of probation, and when you
didn't straighten out, they are now coming down to do
it their way."

Obviously, Bledsoe had been at least partly in the right:
some Northerners, though not all of them, still cher-
ished a desire to see the South remade on the pattern of
the North. And some Southerners—whether rednecks
or not—continued to live in constant dread of Yankeefication. Both the desire and the dread are old, old themes
in American history. They had impressed themselves
upon me in the course of my long study of carpetbaggers, whose basic aim in Reconstruction was, in truth, to
Northernize the South. Hence my choice of a subject for
these lectures, a historical subject that had proved to be
a topic of the times.

In my investigation of the subject of Northernization I
have found certain continuities in it but have also come
upon a number of inconsistencies, ambiguities, and un-
certainties. The South may be eternal, but what "the
South" means is not always clear. Even its boundaries
are uncertain. They change with the passage of years,
and at any particular time they vary according to the
viewpoints of different speakers and writers, who seldom bother to define precisely the region to which they
are referring. The region may consist of all the antebellum slave states, or only those that seceded and joined
the Confederacy. It may or may not include Oklahoma
or West Virginia. It may divide into the Southeast and
the Southwest, or it may merge into the so-called Sun
Belt and cease to have any definite western limit. It may
or may not coincide with the "Census South," the area
that the federal census-takers mark off for their own

purposes. However various or vague the territorial extent, I have not been in the least deterred by second thoughts about it, but have gone right ahead on the fairly safe assumption that the South, after all, is not so much a place as it is an idea.

There is a similar though less serious difficulty in defining the North. From time to time commentators have drawn distinctions between New England and the Middle Atlantic states, between the Northeast and the Northwest, and so on. Although there has appeared to be a variety of Norths, this difficulty has deterred me even less than the preceding one. Whether considered as a nation or as a notion, the North, at least in the most common usage of my Southern spokesmen, consists of everything that is not Southern. It is simply the rest of the country.

What does it mean to "Northernize" the South? Those concerning themselves with the question have, implicitly or explicitly, given various answers to it. Some, but not all, have thought the South would be like the North as soon as blacks ceased to be enslaved, or segregated, or disfranchised, or concentrated in the one part of the country. Some have assumed that the desired or dreaded change would come as an inevitable consequence if ever industrialization and urbanization should arrive—but others have believed that only through industrialization could the South gain sufficient economic strength to preserve its cultural independence. Some have expected the transformation to require, on the part of Northerners, a conscious and organized effort to inculcate their distinctive values, either through control of education or, after migrating to the South in large numbers, through the force of their example. Whatever the process, the result to be anticipated has been, in reality, not so much a South resembling the North as a South conforming to the modern world. Northernization has generally been synonymous with modernization.

Any discussion of regional character is likely to involve a consideration of national character and the relation of the one to the other. On this point, too, there has been both a divergence and an inconsistency of views. On a recent questionnaire a group of Southern college students categorized various traits as "Southern," "Northern," and "American." What they marked as Northern and American characteristics were essentially the same, but the Southern and American were not. That is to say, these Southerners looked upon themselves as deviating from the national norm. Throughout the history of the United States, Northerners have generally looked upon Southerners the same way—that is, as deviants. But Southerners have not always agreed. From time to time they have insisted that *they*, and not the Northerners, were the standard, genuine Americans.

Since I am dealing with beliefs, I have accepted them as such, without questioning their validity except in a few glaring instances. It does not follow that unquestioned beliefs are necessarily congruent with the facts. We are told, for example, on the highest scholarly authority, that the Southern character is distinguished by an attachment to place and an attachment to the past. Presumably Southerners, to a much higher degree than Northerners, are emotionally tied to locality, to the native heath, to home. But the record of two centuries shows that Southerners, as much as Northerners, have been ready to follow the frontier and, even more than Northerners, have been willing to cross the Mason-Dixon line. Millions of Southerners have abandoned home and heath in search of opportunity afar. When appraising Southern character, we must take into account those who left as well as those who stayed behind.

Equally doubtful is the supposition that Southerners are distinguished by a sense of history, a devotion to the past. The past to which they have turned is more mythological than historical. It could be argued that Southerners, while more taken with tradition, have been less interested in history than New Englanders or Midwesterners have been. Large, well supported, highly active historical societies in such states as Massachusetts and Wisconsin long antedate comparable groups in any Southern state. For most of the last two hundred years, historical scholarship has had much more scope in the North than in the South.

One of the most enduring and dubious propositions is that white Southerners constitute an ethnic group, an oppressed minority, a submerged nationality. From time immemorial, Southerners have compared the South to Ireland, Poland, and other countries of that kind. Lately some scholars have discovered close similarities between Americans of recent immigrant background and Southerners of old British stock. Two imaginative historians, Forrest McDonald and Grady McWhiney, have pressed ethnicity to the point of using it, quite literally, to explain what they take to be the basic differences between North and South in antebellum days. Northerners, they say, were predominantly Anglo-Saxon, Southerners predominantly Celtic. In fact, however, Southern whites have lacked essential elements of a true ethnic group: a different genetic or social heritage, a separate language, a unifying religion, and a history of national independence. It hardly answers to refer to the theory of Celtic origin, the peculiarities of the Southern accent, the prevalence of born-again Baptists, or the four brief years of the Confederate States of America.

Still, it must be conceded that parallels do exist between self-conscious Southernism, whether past or present, and the "white ethnic" chauvinism of today. Both manifestations undoubtedly provide emotional gratification and self-esteem for true believers. And in both cases the believers come to feel oppressed, to find some solace in imagining bygone greatness, and to resist full psychological assimilation with the American people. The most significant parallel, however, is this: both kinds of self-identification, ethnic and sectional, are kept alive by artificial respiration. They persist mainly through the efforts of those who have a vested interest in the maintenance of such identities: preachers or priests, politicians, publicists, and professors.

At no time in American history has either the North or the South spoken with a single voice. Never have all Northerners favored the Northernization of the South; never have all Southerners opposed it. Its advocates I might term *Northernists,* and those who have feared it and most insisted that the South was fundamentally different and must be kept so—the professional Southerners—I might call *Southernists.* I doubt if anyone could accurately, or even approximately, gauge the number of Northernists and Southernists at any particular time; certainly I have made no attempt at quantification. But when the two were at their strongest, their influence could be measured by events. The Southernists were numerous and powerful enough to bring about the secession of eleven states, and the Northernists were strong enough to see that Congress passed the Reconstruction Act of 1867. Since the end of Reconstruction the Northernists have seldom numbered more than a handful and have never launched another Northernization movement—unless the civil rights movement of the 1960s can be so construed. Yet Southernists have remained fairly numerous and at times have been quite fervid.

I can only marvel at the persistence of the idea that the South is unique in fundamental ways, that the North is a standing threat to Southern uniqueness, and that good Southerners must ever guard against the Northern peril. This supposed danger has been the concern of a long line of notable Southerners who agreed on it if on nothing else. The list includes Thomas Jefferson (in old age), George Fitzhugh, James D. B. De Bow, Thomas Dixon, Jr., the Nashville Agrarians, Wilbur J. Cash, Louis D. Rubin, Jr., and C. Vann Woodward.

I myself am inclined to agree with those other Southerners who have believed that cultural differences between North and South are minimal, and that these could be further lessened with no real loss to either side. This list is shorter but nevertheless respectable; it includes Hinton Rowan Helper, Henry W. Grady, Walter Hines Page, Howard W. Odum, Charles G. Sellers, and Frank E. Smith. The point is not, of course, that Southerners either have been or ought to be exactly like Northerners. When I think of Southern accents, Southern cooking, and Southern women, I say: *"Vive la différence!"* The question is one of basic values, and it seems to me that, in respect to these, both Northerners and Southerners (with few exceptions) have been typically American all along.

ONE

Two Civilizations—or One?
1780s–1850s

By 1861 THE UNITED STATES HAD COME TO BE DIVIDED into two distinct peoples, two distinct civilizations, one in the North and the other in the South. That, at least, was the belief of many Americans and of many foreigners as well. Observers disagreed as to which of the two civilizations was the more worthy and which the more likely to prevail. Some Northerners, though by no means all of them, had convinced themselves that sooner or later the two should and would become one—that the South must conform to the pattern of the North. Most Southerners were determined to preserve, if not also to propagate, their peculiar ways along with their peculiar institution. To avoid Northernization, they finally undertook to set up a separate country.

Before a demand for remaking the South could arise, there had to be the idea that Southerners were essentially different. This idea existed at least as early as the founding of the republic. Thomas Jefferson expressed it soon after the Revolutionary War when, describing the character of the American people, he used a series of antonyms to contrast them North and South: "cool,"

"fiery"; "sober," "voluptuary"; "laborious," "indolent";
"persevering," "unsteady"; "interested," "generous";
"chicaning," "candid." Jefferson thought these qualities
grew "weaker and weaker by gradation from North to
South and South to North," with Pennsylvania midway
in both geography and character.[1] Thus, in his view, the
American people did not yet fall into one or the other
of two discrete sectional groups.

When the Constitutional Convention met in 1787, the
delegates exhibited a good deal of sectional feeling.
Generally they talked as if there were three geographical
categories of states: the Southern (Maryland, Virginia,
the Carolinas, and Georgia), the Northern or Eastern
(New Hampshire, Massachusetts, Connecticut, and Rhode
Island), and the Middle (New York, New Jersey, Pennsylvania, and Delaware). Men from each section showed
a strong sense of identity with their own part of the
country and an even stronger sense of identity with their
respective states. But those from the Southern states often
spoke as if there were only two sections, and the convention gave signs of a dichotomy, or at least a potential one,
as between North and South.

The Southerners, to be sure, were then far from
unanimous on the subject of slavery. Maryland and Virginia had prohibited slave imports, and North Carolina
had put a fairly high tariff on them, but South Carolina
and Georgia continued to permit and even to encourage
the trade. At Philadelphia, delegates from North and
South Carolina and Georgia threatened that their states
would reject the new constitution if it imposed a ban on
the importation of slaves. George Mason of Virginia argued eloquently in favor of such a provision. "He held
it essential in every point of view," wrote James Madison,
"that the General Government should have power to
prevent the increase of slavery." Slavery discouraged "arts

and manufactures," caused white men to "despise labor,"
prevented the immigration of people who "really enrich
and strengthen a country," and had a "most pernicious
effect on manners," making every master a "petty ty-
rant." Besides, according to Mason, slavery was a wrong
in itself and, as such, would "bring the judgment of
Heaven on a country," for "Providence punishes national sins by national calamities."

The New Englanders did not share the anxiety of this
Virginian. Oliver Ellsworth of Connecticut said that, "as
he had never owned a slave," he "could not judge of the
effects of slavery on character." He could only urge: "Let
us not intermeddle." He and his colleagues from Connecticut and Massachusetts were confident that other
states, South as well as North, would eventually do what
these two states already had done: provide for the abolition of slavery. Then, of course, there would be no need
to worry about sectional differences arising from the
presence or absence of the peculiar institution—and no
need to worry about the prospect of God's vengeance
upon the land.

So far as Mason was concerned, however, neither the
distinctiveness nor the sensitiveness of the South depended on the persistence of slavery. "The *majority* will
be governed by their own interests," he said with reference to the proposed new government. "The Southern
States are the *minority* in both Houses. Is it to be expected that they will deliver themselves bound, hand
and foot, to the Eastern States, and enable them to exclaim, in the words of Cromwell, on a certain occasion—
'the Lord hath delivered them into our hands'?" Presumably the South had to guard against being reduced
to the condition of an Ireland and exposed to the
scourgings of a Cromwell.

With the Virginian George Mason, the South Carolin-

ians Charles Cotesworth Pinckney and Pierce Butler could
agree that the Southern states had mutual concerns quite
apart from the furtherance of slavery. Pinckney listed
five regional economic interests: the fisheries and West
India trade of New England; the general commerce of
New York; the wheat and flour of Pennsylvania and New
Jersey; the tobacco of Maryland, Virginia, and North
Carolina; and the rice and indigo of South Carolina and
Georgia. He refused to concede that this very diversity
would keep one part of the country from using the powers of government to exploit another. Rather, he explained that "his enumeration meant the five minute
interests. It still left the two great divisions, of Northern
and Southern interests." Butler said he considered the
interests of the Southern and Eastern states to be "as
different as the interests of Russia and Turkey"—two
countries that had been warring with one another off
and on for more than two hundred years.

To New Englanders it made little sense to speak of the
Southern states as a minority and the Northern or Eastern states as a majority, or to call the former weak and
the latter strong. After all, the Southern states numbered five and included the most populous of the thirteen—Virginia. The Northern or Eastern totaled only
four if consisting of the New England states, or five if
New York was counted with them.

Nathaniel Gorham of Massachusetts tried to reassure
the worrying Southerners. "He urged the improbability
of a combination against the interest of the Southern
States, the different situations of the Northern and Middle
States being a security against it." Madison conciliatingly
pointed out that Connecticut and New Jersey were (like
the Southern states) predominantly agricultural, not
commercial; that even the "most commercial" of the states
contained a large agricultural interest; and that the

Western states soon to be formed "would be altogether agricultural."

Still, most spokesmen for the South, even at that early date, were and remained convinced that the rest of the country was a threat. The suspicious Southerners agreed to join the new and "more perfect" Union only after obtaining concessions on such matters as the regulation of commerce and the importation of slaves. Pinckney confessed that he had had "prejudices against the Eastern States before he came" to Philadelphia, but had since found the Easterners to be "as liberal and candid as any men whatever." He was sure that "his constituents, though prejudiced against the Eastern States, would be reconciled to [i.e., by] this liberality." The Easterners, or New Englanders (who of course received as well as gave concessions), helped to win over the representatives of the South by the implied promise not to "intermeddle" in its affairs. Thus the new government was made possible by a sectional bargain according to which the South was to be allowed to develop in its own way, differently from the North.[2]

As in the Constitutional Convention, in the first session of the new Congress there were hints of a future North-South confrontation. State pride remained strong and sectional alignments uncertain.

The spirit of the time, 1789–90, is reflected in the diary of the plain-spoken senator from Pennsylvania, William Maclay. Senator Maclay felt more loyalty to the Middle region than to the North and more loyalty to his state than to his region. "I have had to bear the chilling cold of the North and the intemperate warmth of the South, neither of which is favorable to the Middle State

from which I come," he wrote. "[Richard Henry] Lee
and [Ralph] Izard, hot as the burning sands of Carolina,
hate us. [John] Adams with all his frigid friends, cool
and wary, bear us no good-will." But Maclay found no
greater good will on the part of his fellow Middle Staters
from New York. "These Yorkers are the vilest of people,"
he complained. The "York malevolence was showing itself in curious caricatures, in ridicule of the Pennsylva-
nians, etc."

Bad though he thought the New Yorkers, Maclay considered the New Englanders even worse. "We Pennsyl-
vanians act as if we believed that God made of one blood
all families of the earth," he told his diary, "but the Eastern people seem to think that he made none but New
England folks." There was "really more republican
plainness and sincere openness of behavior in Pennsylvania than in any other place." The "gentlemen of New
England," by contrast, stood on "punctilio and cere-
mony," put on "stiffened airs," and kept their distance
from strangers because of "a fear of being contaminated
with foreign manners, customs, or vices." He himself
feared the New Englanders and *their* ways. From his
"knowledge of the Eastern character" he concluded that
the New Englanders would use their "commercial influence" to dominate the new government or, failing that,
would scheme to overthrow it.

"It is true," Maclay consoled himself, "that the genius
of Virginia and Maryland is rather averse to exclusive
commerce. The Southern planter is situated on his extensive domain, surrounded with his slaves and depen-
dents, feels diminution and loses his consequence by being
jumbled among brokers and factors." Hence Maclay was
glad that the permanent capital, if it could not be located
on the Susquehanna, was "going to the Potomac," to a
site between Maryland and Virginia. This location might

help to offset the commercial influence and "give a preponderance to the agricultural interest."

While Maclay looked to Maryland and Virginia to counterbalance New England, he had little reason to hope for good from South Carolina or Georgia. In the Pennsylvania view, the senators from the lower South sometimes took positions as troubling as did those of the extreme North. Pennsylvania was "supposed likely to derive most benefit by migrations" and therefore favored a liberal policy with respect to immigration and naturalization. South Carolina and Georgia opposed this as resolutely as New England did, though Maryland was indifferent, Virginia noncommittal, and North Carolina favorable. Maclay explained: "South Carolina and Georgia want people much, but they fear the migrations, and will check them rather than run the chance of importing people who may be averse to slavery."

The slavery issue was already becoming a wedge between Pennsylvania, on the one hand, and South Carolina and Georgia on the other. Pennsylvania had begun the emancipation process for slaves in the commonwealth, and the Quakers' Pennsylvania Abolition Society was demanding that the federal government do the same for slaves in the country at large. New England was not yet particularly sympathetic with the national antislavery cause—or so it seemed to Maclay, who thought that when Vice-President John Adams presented the society's petitions he "did it rather with a sneer." Maclay was left to defend the society and its head, Benjamin Franklin, against attacks from the South Carolina senators, Izard and Butler. "These men have a most settled antipathy to Pennsylvania, owing to the doctrines patronized in that State on the subject of slavery," Maclay noted. "Pride makes fools of them, or rather completes what Nature began."[3]

➢➢❯❮❮❮

A generation later the *bête noire* of slaveowners was New England rather than Pennsylvania, and slaves were confined (with very few exceptions) to the states old and new that lay below the Mason-Dixon line and the Ohio River. Where to run the slave-and-free-state demarcation beyond the Mississippi became a matter of serious dispute when Missouri applied for admission as a slave state. The Missouri controversy of 1819–1821 resulted from, and contributed to, an intensifying North-South polarity. It also raised, in a fairly explicit form, the question whether Northern character and culture ought not to prevail throughout the land.

In the course of the congressional debate on Missouri, New Hampshire's Senator David L. Morril expressed his concern for the future of the expanding country. "Will its intellectual and moral improvements progress and keep pace with its rapid population [growth] and increasing wealth?" Morril feared that the "uncontrolled extension of involuntary servitude" would "impair all those virtuous qualities" that formed the "stamina, nerve, muscle, and hope of the nation." Slavery, he argued, tended not only to lessen a country's moral and physical strength but also to retard its industrial development and corrupt its polity, causing a degeneration from democracy to aristocracy and even to despotism.

To clinch the argument, Morril quoted statements that Jefferson had published in his *Notes on the State of Virginia* (1787)—statements very similar to those that Jefferson's fellow Virginian George Mason had made to the Constitutional Convention in the same year. "There must doubtless be an unhappy influence on the manners of our people, produced by the existence of slavery among us," Jefferson had written. "The whole commerce be-

tween master and slave is a perpetual exercise in the
most boisterous passions, the most unremitting despotism on the one part, and degrading submission on the
other." The result, according to Jefferson, was to destroy
the industriousness along with the morals of the whites,
while brutalizing the blacks. "Indeed, I tremble for my
country when I reflect that God is just. . . ."

Southern senators bridled at Morril's remarks. "The
honorable gentleman from New Hampshire . . . has been
pleased to draw a parallel between the inhabitants of the
different sections of the country," Freeman Walker, of
Georgia, protested, " . . . in which he has not failed to
give a very decided preference to those who inhabit States
in which slavery is not tolerated; and . . . has ascribed
this vast and essential difference to the influence of slavery." While Walker was willing to admit that the people
of Morril's section were "brave, virtuous, moral, religious, and patriotic," he insisted that those were not sectional qualities and that the inhabitants of the slaveholding
states would not suffer by comparison in respect to those
qualities or in respect to benevolence, humanity, and democracy. After all, a slaveholder had "penned the im-
mortal Declaration of Independence." As for that same
author's *Notes on the State of Virginia*, Senator William
Smith of South Carolina brushed aside those "observations of Mr. Jefferson," calling them "the effusions of the
speculative philosophy of his young and ardent mind
. . . which his riper years have corrected."[4]

Regarding the effect of slavery upon the slaveowner's
character, Secretary of State John Quincy Adams es-
poused the same view that Jefferson earlier had expressed. After talking with his cabinet colleague John C.
Calhoun, Adams thought he saw the character of Southerners in a new light. "The discussion of this Missouri
question has betrayed the secret of their souls," he re-

corded in his diary. "In the abstract they admit that slavery is an evil. . . . But when probed to the quick upon it, they show at the bottom of their souls pride and vainglory in their condition of masterdom. They fancy themselves more generous and noble-hearted than the plain freemen who labor for subsistence. They look down upon the simplicity of a Yankee's manners, because he has no habits of overbearing like theirs and cannot treat negroes like dogs." Adams went on to note that slavery "taints the very sources of moral principles" and "establishes false estimates of virtue and vice." He thought the "bargain between freedom and slavery contained in the Constitution" was "morally and politically vicious," and he wondered whether the free states ought not to form a new Union "unpolluted with slavery, with a great and glorious object to effect, namely, that of rallying to their standard the other States by the universal emancipation of their slaves."[5] Then the country would be whole again, and the South would be essentially like the North.

The Missouri controversy also reawakened Jefferson—"like a fire bell in the night"—but to a very different consciousness from that of Adams. Jefferson's "riper years" had indeed "corrected" his earlier opinions. Laying out the University of Virginia, he became preoccupied with higher education, and he was appalled to learn of the large number of Southern youths attending Northern colleges. There they would get "lessons of anti-Missourianism," and they would probably return home "deeply impressed with the sacred principles of our holy alliance of Restrictionists"—that is, advocates of restricting the spread of slavery. Southern parents could no longer trust Northern professors, who were in a position to "fashion to their own form the minds and affections" of the young. So Jefferson conceived a new mission for his university. Originally his chief aim had been to pro-

mote the freedom of the intellect; now it was to defend
the ideology of slavery. From all over the South, fathers
wrote to thank him for making it unnecessary for them
to send their sons to the North.

At the time of the Missouri dispute other Southerners
besides Jefferson feared the South was being exposed to
contamination from Northern teachers and teachings.
A South Carolinian urged that South Carolina College
fill vacancies with native professors. If, this man argued,
"our selection of Teachers and Principal is made from
those quarters of the union which usually supply the
demand, we shall incur the risk of having sentiments
inculcated in the minds of our youth extremely dangerous to the interests and prosperity of the Southern States."
The Kentucky legislature considered a bill to exclude
Yankee peddlers from Kentucky, and one member proposed also to exclude such a "spiritual pedlar" as the
Yankee president of Transylvania University.[6]

The Missouri crisis was something of a rehearsal for
the sectional crises that were to follow in 1832–1833,
1849–1850, and 1860–1861. All of them heightened,
on one side of the dividing line, the hope and demand
for Southern conformity to Northern standards and, on
the other side, the fear of such a result and the determination to resist it.

➤➤❌◀◀

In the antebellum period it was not clear whether Americans had yet developed, or would ever develop, what
could properly be called a national character. Perhaps
they possessed and would continue to possess only a regional character, depending on the part of the country
they lived in. The question attracted the interest of Europeans who traveled in and wrote about the United

States from the 1820s to the 1850s. These observers
agreed at least that character and culture varied consid-
erably from region to region. Since they derived their
opinions largely from Americans, the Europeans reflected not only their own observations and prejudices
but also the perceptions that Northerners and Southerners had of themselves and of each other. Native commentators generally showed as much or more partiality
when they gave direct expression to their views. As a
Hungarian visitor noted, "The two great portions of the
United States rail at one another very unscrupulously,
more than any foreigners could do; and yet they are
very touchy if any remark is made [by a foreigner] which
does not imply admiration."[7]

Most foreigners found little to approve in slavery but
much to admire in the slaveowner. They saw him as quite
different from the Northerner, especially the New Englander, though few drew the contrast quite as starkly as
did Thomas Hamilton, a gentleman from Scotland who
had a fellow feeling for the gentlemen of the Southern
states. "The poles are not more diametrically opposed
than a native of the States south of the Potomac and a
New-Englander," Hamilton wrote in 1833.

They differ in everything of thought, feeling, and opinion. The latter is a man of regular and decorous habits, intelligent, and persevering; phlegmatic in temperament, devoted to the pursuits of gain,
and envious of those who are more successful than himself. The
former—I speak of the opulent and educated—is distinguished by a
high-mindedness, generosity, and hospitality, by no means predica-
ble in his more eastern [i.e., Northern] neighbours. He values money
only for the enjoyment it can procure, is fond of gaiety, given to
social pleasures, somewhat touchy and choleric, and as eager to avenge
an insult as to show a kindness. . . . In point of manner, the Southern
gentlemen are decidedly superior to all others of the Union.

In point of honesty, it seemed to Hamilton, the New
Englander ranked at the very bottom. "The whole race

of Yankee pedlars, in particular, are proverbial for their dishonesty," he reported. "They warrant broken watches to be the best time-keepers in the world; sell pinch-beck trinkets for gold; and have always a large assortment of wooden nutmegs, and stagnant barometers."[8]

Southerners accepted without question the compliments of Hamilton and other Europeans, but indignantly rejected even the slightest imputation, such as the suggestion that some men and women of the planter class were "languid." Spokesmen for the planters polished a flattering image. "Domestic slavery in the Southern States has produced the same results in elevating the character of the master that it did in Greece and Rome," the Virginian George Fitzhugh declared. "He is lofty and independent in his sentiments, generous, affectionate, brave and eloquent; he is superior to the Northerner in every thing but the arts of thrift."[9]

Preachers, politicians, and publicists led the slaveless farmer to believe that he, too, possessed the fine qualities that distinguished the planter from the Yankee. James D. B. De Bow, of *De Bow's Review*, published in New Orleans, intimated that such was the fact in reviewing one of the travel books of the Connecticut-born Frederick Law Olmsted. "This simple faith in the meanness of the people of the North, and especially of New England," Olmsted replied, "is no eccentricity of Mr. De Bow's. It is in accordance with the general tone of literature and of conversation at the South, that penuriousness, disingenuousness, knavish cunning, cant, cowardice, and hypocrisy are assumed to be the prevailing traits by which they [New Englanders] are distinguished from the people of the South—not the poor people of New England from the planters of the South, but the people generally from the people generally."[10]

Just as Southerners broadened the scope of the planter

ideal to include more than the planter class, so they widened the application of the Yankee stereotype to include more than the people of New England. As the Alabamian Daniel R. Hundley pointed out, foreigners applied the term "Yankee" to all Americans, Southerners as well as Northerners. Southerners "would not consent to have the name applied to themselves," but used it for Northerners in general. Northerners limited it to New Englanders. The "New-Yorker becomes quite indignant if you call him a *Yankee*," Hundley wrote, "and so do the Keystoners [Pennsylvanians], and the people who live in our Western States. Yankee with all these is looked upon usually as a term of reproach—signifying a shrewd, sharp, chaffering, oily-tongued, soft-sawdering, inquisitive, money-making, money-saving, and money-worshipping individual."[11] It was certainly a term of reproach as Southerners employed it. "A 'Yankee' is perhaps the most contemptuous name a Southern [*sic*] can apply to any man," an Englishman observed. "It implies with him every dirty passion; cowardice, greed, hypocrisy, and every vile quality."[12]

Another Englishman, visiting New England, noted: "This term is not deemed reproachful here; persons often boast of their being Yankees, as implying a more thorough English descent, with a less admixture of foreign blood."[13] That was in 1841, when the Irish were only beginning to arrive in large numbers; already the Protestants of old stock were calling themselves Yankees in contradistinction to non-Protestant newcomers. To native New Englanders the word had positive connotations of industry, literacy, sobriety, morality, and sound religion.

New Englanders and other Northerners traveling in the South sometimes discovered the hospitality and charm

that Europeans praised. But the Northerners also found
other traits that suggested the prevalence of a split personality—or the existence of two quite different but
equally typical personalities. Southerners had a "custom
of carrying arms," showed a "tendency to personal violence," and indulged in frequent "shooting scrapes." Still,
the Maine abolitionist John Abbott thought he would
like to live among the people he met on his Southern
trip in 1859: "They seem kind, generous, warm-hearted."
Abbott wondered if there was "another class" whom he
never had a chance to meet but whose editorials and
speeches he often read in the newspapers. "Is it possible
that the worst part of the slave-holders, with bowie-knives
and revolvers, have over-awed the conscientious portion
of the community?"[14]

This Maine native also approved what he considered
a comparative absence of racism among Southern whites.
"I am struck with the kindness with which the white
population address the negroes, and the manifestly
friendly relations which generally exist between the two
classes," he wrote. "The Negrophobia at the North is
unknown at the South." Earlier, on the basis of an American visit in the 1830s, the young Frenchman Alexis de
Tocqueville had observed: "The prejudice of the race
appears to be stronger in the States which have abolished slavery than in those where it still exists; and nowhere is it so intolerant as in those States where servitude
never has been known." English travelers usually considered the black to be at least as bad off in the North as in
the South. One said the Negro was treated like a dog in
both sections, the only difference being that "in the South
he is sometimes a pet dog, whereas in the North he is
always a cur, kicked and booted on every occasion." A
Hungarian noticed that "the condition of the free-

coloured people in the North" was "as much decried in
the South as the treatment of the Southern slaves [was
decried] in the North."[15]

Northerners took a dimmer and dimmer view of
Southern character as sectional feeling intensified during the prewar decades. Ralph Waldo Emerson, for one,
went from grudging admiration to utter detestation. After
his graduation in 1821, Emerson wrote to a Southern
classmate that he wanted to investigate the "peculiar and
striking distinctions" that he had seen "separating our
Northern and Southern countrymen" at Harvard. In
the 1840s, after traveling in the South, he deduced that
the Southerner acquired self-reliance from his way of
life. "The Southerner has personality, has temperament,
has manners, persuasion, address, and terror." The "cold
Yankee" had none of that attractive fire. But Emerson
concluded that the typical Southerner was a mere "ani-
mal," one to whom life had little meaning or value, after
the South Carolina Congressman Preston Brooks broke
a cane on the head of the Massachusetts Senator Charles
Sumner in 1856.[16]

As bad as his proclivity for bullying—or even worse,
in the eyes of bourgeois Northerners—was the Southerner's lack of enterprise and thrift. It was a shock to
find in the South so much "idleness & extravagance,"
"luxury & sloth," "reckless expenditure," and "foolish
dissipation." Tocqueville saw the Ohioan and the Kentuckian as typifying Northern and Southern attitudes
toward business and work. The Ohioan showed an "av-
idity in the pursuit of gain" that amounted to "a species
of heroism," while the Kentuckian scorned labor and
coveted wealth "much less than pleasure and excite-
ment." There was, in short, "a very striking difference
between the commercial capacity of the inhabitants of
the South and those of the North."

According to Tocqueville, the land reflected this difference in the aptitudes of the people. In "shipping, manufactures, railroads, and canals," the Northern states were far ahead of the Southern. The contrast could be seen all along the Ohio River and the Mason-Dixon line—on the one side, "progress and prosperity"; on the other, "comparative poverty and gloom." Other foreigners agreed that the South was, relatively speaking, very backward and very poor. Calling the region "the Ireland of America," an Englishman noted: "Everything appears slovenly, ill-arranged, incomplete, windows do not shut, doors do not fasten." Both Northerners and Europeans mentioned the ubiquitous signs of decay: dilapidated houses, sedge-covered fields, weed-grown gardens, and gullied slopes. "How different from the face of a New England State, dotted over with neat farm-houses."[17]

Essentially, as some saw it, the difference between North and South was the difference between the modern and the obsolete. While the one region was up to date, the other was no better than feudal, according to the Massachusetts antislavery orator Wendell Phillips. "The South is the thirteenth and fourteenth centuries," Phillips declared in 1837. Twenty years later the Englishman James Stirling got much the same impression when he returned to New York after a Southern tour: "The little step from South to North is a stride from barbarism to civilization; a leap from the sixteenth to the nineteenth century."

Most critics blamed slavery for the slothfulness of Southerners and the backwardness of the South. "I could easily prove," Tocqueville asserted, "that almost all the differences which may be remarked between the characters of Americans in the Southern and in the Northern States originated in slavery." Some observers, both hostile and friendly ones, traced the cause back to the

presumed Puritan and Cavalier origins of Northern and
Southern colonists. Stirling argued that the "difference
in the nature of the two peoples" had "caused the difference in their domestic institutions"—rather than the other
way around. From the first settlements, from Plymouth
Rock and Jamestown, a Vermont newspaper contended,
"American civilization" had "streamed across the continent on parallel or nearly parallel lines" and in two distinct forms, the one industrious and democratic, the other
indolent and aristocratic. Some commentators referred
to geographical influence, to regional variations of climate and soil, but few, if any, thought the unprogressive-
ness was due to deficiencies in natural resources. The
South seemed "richly endowed by nature" and "wonder-
fully adapted to be the home of opulence, intelligence,
refinement, and joy." Surely the South could advance at
least as fast and as far as the North—were it not for the
character of the Southern people and the peculiarity of
their institutions.[18]

Writers of the prewar decades occasionally described
three or more regional types in the United States, but
much more often they assumed or implied that basically
there were only two. By 1860–1861 the dichotomy was
fairly complete—Northerners and Southerners—and
each claimed to be the real and typical Americans. Abbott told Southerners: there has been "a change on *your*
part and not on *ours*"; you have forgotten the "lessons
of liberty" that George Washington, Thomas Jefferson,
and other Revolutionary patriots taught; we Northerners "still entertain these same sentiments which were en-
tertained by the founders of our republic." But De Bow
pointed to the polyglot North, with its hordes of immigrants, and contrasted it with the South and the comparatively few and "select" foreigners. "Our people
partake of the true American character," De Bow in-

sisted, "and are mainly the descendants of those who fought the battles of the Revolution."[19] If Americans had indeed acquired a national character at the time of the Revolutionary War, either Northerners or Southerners or both had apparently lost it by the time of the Civil War.

On the basis of his observations in the 1830s, Tocqueville predicted that sooner or later Southerners would be practically identical with Northerners. As Americans intermingled more and more, he explained, "the differences resulting from their climate, their origin, and their institutions" would become less and less. Northerners were constantly moving to the South; they were responsible for almost all the "commercial operations" in that region. "This continual emigration of the North to the South is peculiarly favorable to the fusion of all the provincial characters into one national character," Tocqueville reasoned. "The civilization of the North appears to be the common standard, to which the whole nation will one day be assimilated."[20] In saying this, Tocqueville may or may not have been foretelling the distant future, but he was certainly a poor prophet with respect to the next few decades.

True, thousands of the Northern-born resided in the South during this period. Many engaged in business (in the "commercial operations" that Tocqueville referred to) or in planting or merely farming. Some achieved prominence as merchants, bankers, manufacturers, clergymen, college professors or presidents, newspaper editors, lawyers, legislators, or judges. These men, however, exerted little or no distinctive and positive Northern influence upon the South. Instead, they accepted and endorsed, or at any rate conformed to, the regional mores. Other newcomers from the North—those who persisted in criticizing slavery or the society based on it— were soon driven out.

Conflicting loyalties could be poignant for a Northerner living in the South, as they were for Seargent S. Prentiss. A young man in the 1820s, he moved from Maine to Mississippi and soon rose to fame as one of the South's, and the nation's, most electrifying orators. At first Prentiss preferred the Northern "manner of living" to the Southern, and he disapproved of slavery, but before long he was defending Southern institutions and interests. Eventually he married a Mississippi planter's daughter and fathered four children by her. Still, he always retained a sentimental attachment to his native New England, where his beloved mother and sister continued to reside. He was a Unionist whose Unionism came from the heart. "In the veins of our children flows Northern and Southern blood; how shall it be separated?" he asked as he addressed the New England Society of New Orleans in 1845. "We love the land of our adoption, so do we that of our birth. Let us ever be true to both." Four years later, in the midst of the sectional crisis of 1849–1850, he was beginning to wonder whether he or anyone else could be true to both North and South much longer. Again addressing the New England Society, he stirringly warned against "the incalculable woes that would follow disunion," but he "concluded with the remark that, if such a calamity was coming, he could only cast in his lot with the land of his wife and children."[21]

Like converts in general, Northern converts to the Southern cause often strove to outdo the birthright believers in exhibitions of faith. Daniel R. Hundley hardly exaggerated when he thus characterized the Yankee who went South to live: "Notwithstanding he may have been previously a constant employe on the Underground Railroad, he immediately discovers a sweet divinity in the peculiar institution, and no Southern overseer could expatiate more eloquently on its manifold beauties than he." Thomas Cooper, once an antislavery youth, moved from Pennsylvania to South Carolina to take a position as a college professor and soon attained prominence as an advocate of slavery and nullification. Albert Pike and F. A. P. Barnard, New Englanders living in the South, one as an editor and the other as an educator, were leaders in the campaign for economic independence from the North. Barnard declared in 1851: "At present, the North fattens and grows rich on the South." John A. Quitman, a Mississippian from New York, stood out among the "fire-eaters" as an early and extreme secessionist. Daniel Pratt, the New Hampshire native who built a great industrial complex in Alabama, opposed secession but supported the Confederacy and pledged his economic resources to it. Approximately fifty men of Northern birth attained the rank of general in the Confederate army.[22]

It would appear that the Northerners who migrated to the South in the antebellum period seldom acted as missionaries of Northern culture. In any case, they were far outnumbered by the Southerners who migrated to the North. The 1850 census showed roughly three times as many of the latter as of the former—more than 600,000 natives of the slave states residing in the free states, only about 200,000 natives of the free states residing in the slave states.[23]

It seemed more likely, at least to some Northerners, that the Southern migrants would corrupt the North than that the Northern migrants would civilize the South. It boded ill for the North that "sluggish and inanimate" people from Virginia and the Carolinas, instead of "enterprising" people from New England, should have settled southern Ohio, Indiana, and Illinois. "It is unquestionable," a Maine native editorialized, "that the immigration from the South has brought into the free states more ignorance, poverty, and thriftlessness than an equal amount of European immigration."

Generally those Ohio, Indiana, and Illinois settlers had moved northwestward because they disliked the slave system or disliked the slaveowners; they were fugitives from the slavery-based society of the South. If *they* constituted a threat to Northern civilization, how much greater a menace must have loomed from the Southerners who demanded the right to migrate with their slaves! These Southerners would carry their barbaric institution and customs into the hitherto unspoiled territories of the West. Northerners would then be unable to expand their own society with its enterprise, its opportunities, its social mobility. As the Englishman Stirling said of the "free North" in 1856: "It fears that Southern aggression will wrest from the free North those rich territories where she hoped to find a profitable field for labour and capital, and a useful safety-valve for political discontent."

Abolitionists and free-soilers feared that Southerners might impose their laws and customs upon the Northern states as well as upon the Western territories. After Southern legislatures had appealed to Northern ones to suppress antislavery agitation, Congressman John Quincy Adams said in 1842 that he saw "a settled system and purpose" on the part of Southerners "to destroy all the principles of civil liberty in the free States, not for the purpose of preserving their institutions within their own limits, but to force their detested principles of slavery into all the free States." Ex-Governor William H. Seward of New York, who had grand imperial aspirations for the United States, declared in 1845 that the question whether slavery should be restricted and eventually abolished was the question whether the "free and vigorous North and West" should "work out the welfare of the country, and drag the reluctant South up to participate in the same glorious destinies."[24]

The abolitionists and the free-soilers saw themselves as standing upon the defensive: to them, the South was the aggressor. Their sense of Southern encroachment sharpened with the political events of the 1850s, particularly the repeal of the Missouri Compromise and the opening of new territory to slavery in 1854. "With a minority of States, with less than a third, thirty-two per cent., of the white population, how is it that the South has managed to appropriate to herself so large a share of official influence and executive power?" After raising this question, the English traveler Stirling went on: "The answer seems to me to be, that the aristocratic nature of Southern society is more fitted for political organization, and therefore the small but compact phalanx of Southern leaders has generally been able to out-manoeuvre the more numerous but less manageable hosts of the North." The Republican party came into existence to marshal these Northern hosts, to resist the advance of the proslavery Southern phalanx, and to prevent the North from being Southernized.

The Republicans grew more and more convinced that, to protect the North, they would have to transform the South. They feared that the two ways of life, the two civilizations, could not long coexist. As early as 1837 Wendell Phillips had said that the spirit of freedom and the spirit of slavery must always contend for absolute mastery: "They cannot live together." In 1858 Abraham Lincoln spoke of the house divided, the house that could not stand that way forever. In the same year Seward introduced the phrase "irrepressible conflict," by which he did not mean inevitable war but did mean that the United States would, "sooner or later, become either entirely a slaveholding nation, or entirely a free-labor nation."

Some Republicans were confident that, once slavery had disappeared, the transformation of the South would follow almost automatically. One of the party's editors opined that "to destroy slavery" was "not to destroy the South, but to change its social organization for the better." Others thought the task would require something more than mere emancipation. According to the *Cincinnati Gazette*, it demanded "the introduction upon Southern territory of the Northern system of life." At least a few believed it would necessitate a mass migration of Northerners, who would carry with them their industrial skills and industrious habits. As the *New York Tribune* argued with respect to one state, "It is only by the abolition of slavery and the cessation of slaveholding and the slave trade, followed by the emigration of Northern capitalists, manufacturers, and merchants, that the practical regeneration of Virginia can be effected." [25]

The South, regenerated, would closely resemble the idealized North of the Republicans. "Give the South a people moderately close settled, moderately well-informed, moderately ambitious, and moderately industrious, somewhat approaching that of Ohio, for instance, and what a business it would have!"—so Olmsted speculated. Abbott wrote eagerly of the possibilities for poor blacks and poor whites to improve themselves as the South realized the Republican ideal of a free-labor, get-ahead society. The slaves would then turn into self-respecting peasants, hired hands, or even farm owners. The slaveless whites would become employers and would "see a new world of hope opening before them. Soon our whole Southern country would exhibit the aspect of cheerful and happy industry which enlivens and blesses the North."[26]

Not all antislavery Northerners contemned slaveowning Southerners. Probably more Northerners got their idea of the South from Harriet Beecher Stowe's *Uncle Tom's Cabin* (1851) than from any other book. Mrs. Stowe presented a sympathetic and charming planter family in the St. Clairs, and she made her most hateful villain, Simon Legree, a Vermonter. She aimed to show the evils of the slave system, not the evils of the Southern people. Other Northern novelists went much further than she did in idealizing the planter class. James Fenimore Cooper and James K. Paulding imagined that its members personified a gentility and a nobility lamentably absent among the materialistic, money-grubbing businessmen of the North.[27] These authors seemed to think the North ought to imitate the South, rather than the reverse.

The most sympathetic and admiring Northerners— the Northern men with Southern principles, the "doughfaces"—were not Republicans but Democrats. If they saw no compelling reason to adopt Southern ways, they saw still less reason to impose Northern ways on the South. In the North a vote for the Democrats was a vote for letting the South stay as it was. A ballot cast for the Republicans indicated a willingness, if not a wish, to see the South remade. And in 1860 the Republicans carried the North so overwhelmingly that, with that region's electoral count alone, their candidate won the presidency of the United States.

While Republicans feared the spread of Southern influence, slaveowners took as great or greater alarm at the
prospective spread of Northern influence. Yankeepho-
bia, long endemic in the South, grew rapidly in viru-
lence. "The entire South," a former Oberlin student noted
on an 1844 tour of the region, "dread and dislike Yankees and laugh not a little at their brogue as they call
it—quite as much as do we northerners at those [i.e.,
that] of the South." Southerners, too, began to believe
there was a conflict that was becoming less and less re-
pressible. "The parties in this conflict are not merely
abolitionists and slaveholders," declaimed the Presbyterian Dr. J. H. Thornwell, soon to be president of South
Carolina College, in the crisis year 1850. "They are athe-
ists, socialists, communists, red republicans, jacobins on
the one side, and the friends of order and regulated
freedom on the other."[28] In response to what Southerners perceived as a rising threat of Northernization, they
turned to the pursuit of economic, cultural, and finally
political independence from the North.

Some opposed or at least hesitated to encourage the
diversification of the Southern economy, for fear that
this in itself would have a Yankeefying effect. It could
menace the very survival of the unique Southern species, according to a Virginian who delivered the 1854
Fourth of July address at the Virginia Military Institute
in Lexington. The "peculiar type of Virginia character,"
the speaker warned, might be "blotted out forever" be-
neath a wave of commercialism and industrialism sweep-
ing down from the North. "Though the State were
covered with improvements, though each half hour were
proclaimed by the warning note of the rushing train—

though populous cities and fertile fields should give us assurance of a mighty prosperity, I should still mourn the loss of that Man and Woman which belong peculiarly to the Southern States."[29]

But others saw in economic development and diversification a means of preserving rather than destroying the South's special character and culture. Even such defenders of Southern principles as John C. Calhoun and his fellow nullificationists had tried to promote such development through the commercial conventions of the 1830s. At the convention of 1839 Robert Y. Hayne blamed federal taxes and expenditures for "diverting to the North the profits of southern capital and labor," "stimulating the commercial industry of the North," "building up northern cities at the expense of those in the South and Southwest," and "depriving us of that DIVERSITY IN THE PURSUITS OF THE PEOPLE" on which prosperity largely depended. "The citizens of the southern and southwestern states, driven from the animating pursuits of commerce, have, it is undeniable, devoted themselves *too exclusively* to agriculture."[30]

The revived commercial conventions of the 1850s devoted themselves to the same program, as did other organizations in the South. They sought to encourage the growth of Southern manufactures, railroads, and shipping lines. If such projects should tend directly or indirectly to Yankeefy the region, concurrent proposals would counteract the tendency. Reformers urged that Southerners elect to office only those candidates "identified with the southern population"; that they cancel subscriptions to Northern periodicals "hostile to our land and institutions"; that they accept none but Southern-born preachers and teachers, endow and patronize home colleges, and stop sending sons and daughters to school

in the North (where their minds were "poisoned"); that
they write and publish Southern textbooks, and vacation
in Southern instead of Northern summer resorts.[31]

Advocates of economic development compared the
South favorably with the North, yet they seemed to envy
Northern progress and to resent Northern self-
satisfaction. "We have heard of the ceaseless industry,
and energy, and enterprise of the *North*, and they have
become proverbial with us," De Bow wrote in a speech
for a New York agricultural and industrial exhibit in
1851. "I will not deny . . . that in my own region I would
imitate very much [of] what belongs to your character
and career; but . . . I am not ashamed to name that region in the same breath with your own . . . so much do I
believe in *substantial* blessings we have the advantage,
that I would be very far indeed from changing places
with you in the confederacy!" But, De Bow continued,
the Northern people seemed to think "the landmarks of
'Mason and Dixon'" were "the very outposts of all civilization and progress." Really, "we of the *benighted* South"
have "nothing to blush for," De Bow insisted, and he
proceeded to detail some of the Southern accomplish-
ments in commerce, industry, and transportation,
prophetically noting that "the South is becoming, and
will become . . . the great *cotton manufacturing region of
the world*."[32]

Even more optimistic and outspoken than De Bow
was the Virginian George Fitzhugh. "Until the last fifteen years," Fitzhugh wrote in *Sociology for the South; or,
The Failure of Free Society* (1854), "our great error was to
imitate Northern habits, customs and institutions. Our
circumstances are so opposite to theirs, that whatever
suits them is almost certain not to suit us." Fortunately,
it seemed to Fitzhugh, Southerners had begun to realize
that slavery was right and their own society the best.

Slave society was exempt from the ills that afflicted free society in Europe and America—exempt from the strikes, riots, and other disorders that were "occasioned by the absence of domestic slavery." And what remedy was "so obvious as to remove the cause of those diseases by restoring that institution?" Instead of the South following the North's example, the North ought to follow the South's. Fitzhugh professed to believe that it would soon do so; "towards slavery," he maintained, "the North and all Western Europe are unconsciously marching." While the North struggled with its handicaps, the South was making real and steady progress. "Every day more and more is done for education, the mechanic arts, manufactures and internal improvements," he boasted. "We will soon be independent of the North."[33]

Fitzhugh pressed the counterattack on a lecturing visit to the North in 1855. So, too, in the 1850s, did other prominent Southerners, among them the politicians Robert Toombs, Howell Cobb, and R. M. T. Hunter and the novelist and poet William Gilmore Simms. Their lectures stressed the beauties of life on the Southern plantation and contrasted them with the evils of existence in the Northern city, amidst filth, poverty, and crime. Meanwhile the newspapers and magazines of the South kept repeating the same message of Southern virtue and Northern vice.[34]

A notable dissenter was Hinton Rowan Helper, a self-described "true hearted southerner" whose ancestors had "resided in North Carolina between one hundred and two hundred years." In *The Impending Crisis of the South* (1857) Helper agreed that the South ought to achieve economic independence. "Nearly all the profits," he complained, "accrue to the North, and are there invested in the erection of those magnificent cities and stupendous works of art which dazzle the eyes of the

South." He disagreed, however, about the extent of
Southern progress and about the means of furthering
it. He hoped yet to elevate his home region "to an equality, socially, morally, intellectually, industrially, politically,
and financially," and he thought the way to do that was
to get rid of slavery, whose "pestilential atmosphere" he
blamed for the South's "inanition and slothfulness," its
"wretchedness and desolation," its "melancholy inactiv-
ity and dilapidation."

Helper welcomed Northerners and their ways. "Our
Northern cousins," he declared, taking a cue from the
New York Tribune, "'do not hate the South, war on the
South, nor seek to ruin the South'; on the contrary, they
love our particular part of the nation, and . . . they would
promote its interests by facilitating the abolition of slavery." Helper saw so nearly eye to eye with the Republicans that they distributed his book as party propaganda
throughout the North. He thought of himself primarily
as a liberator of the South's "poor white persons," all of
whom were "regarded with less esteem and attention
than negroes," and "vast numbers" of whom were "infi-
nitely worse off."[35] If many of his fellow non-slaveholding
farmers were susceptible to his appeal, very few had a
chance to show it, since the book was almost totally sup-
pressed throughout the South.

The fears of Southerners, already high, rose to a hys-
terical pitch at the news, in 1859, of John Brown's raid
on Harpers Ferry. This looked like the penultimate move
in a Northern conspiracy to take over the South. Southerners now went to extremes in an effort to eliminate
the danger of Yankee contamination. Mobs fell upon
strangers whom they suspected of being Northern in
origin or sympathy. Students and others residing or visiting in the North returned hastily to their homes. As
the months passed, the panic continued, and it gained

additional stimulus from Lincoln's election. Secession and the formation of the Confederacy followed as a last-ditch attempt to quarantine the South against the plague of Yankeeism.

In the minds of its advocates, the Southern independence movement was not merely a way of escaping Northern influence; rather, it was a way of realizing at last the full potentiality of the Southern spirit. Southerners had been fundamentally different from Northerners all along, a Mississippian explained in *De Bow's Review* during the secession winter. At the time of the American Revolution there already existed on this continent "two systems of civilization," "two distinct peoples," "two separate nationalities." It was impossible for the new government under the Constitution to reconcile the two. Society, regardless of government, "remains always the same," and so do "the character, feelings, and wants of the beings who compose it." The "political constitution" becomes "a mere nullity, when its action is made to repress the vital forces of the social life." Soon these forces would be released for Southerners, who thus were more fortunate than some contemporary Europeans. "Hungary, Ireland, and Poland have still left them a social life, but where is their once proud nationality? Lost in that universal and inevitable doom that awaits all *minority sections* of powerful empire, that prefer union to independence—servitude to freedom."

"The idea of Southern inferiority has become so deeply rooted that it has become part of our nature," a Virginian wrote in the same magazine in 1861, "and nothing but the struggles of the revolution now in progress will pluck it out of our hearts. This fatal idea, which, like the deadly Upas, has blighted Southern commerce, manufactures and literature, is the result of our own folly. We placed the education of the young—the mould-

ing of thought and opinion—in the hands of our enemies. . . . We have expelled the whole brood of them
["peripatetic Yankees" formerly teaching in the South],
and we are fast eradicating the false sentiments and ideas
which they introduced and labored so assiduously to impress upon the minds of the young." Henceforth, in the
independent South, commerce and manufactures and
literature could be expected to flourish.[36]

For the time being, Northern Democrats generally
sympathized with the revolutionary Southerners. The
Democratic Standard of Concord, New Hampshire, insisted that the North must "acknowledge the equality of
the South" and recognize and respect "her constitution
of society and her forms of civilization." The *Cincinnati
Press* accepted the contention of secessionists that their
"hostility to a Union with the North" went "to the very
sentiments, opinions, abstract principles and even religion of the people," and that hence the only alternatives
were "a peaceable separation, or a bloody civil war"—a
war that could "have no other end but in separation." So
Democrats continued to question both the propriety and
the practicability of imposing Northern culture upon
the South.

Some Republicans were momentarily inclined to accept disunion and to shed slavery by shedding the slave
states. But other party members never considered letting the seceders go in peace, and the firing on Fort
Sumter brought an end to the idea not only among Republicans but also among most Northern Democrats. The
Burlington Times, a Vermont paper that had campaigned
for Lincoln, now reminded its readers of the historic
contrast between the "spirit of arrogance and domination" of the Southerners and the "plainness and reverent spirit of the Puritans," whose descendants the
Southerners despised as Yankees. "Massachusetts must

go down to Virginia, or Virginia come up to Massachu-setts," the newspaper proclaimed. "As God reigns Virginia must come to Massachusetts, and there shall be *one people*."[37] Ironically, in attempting to escape Northern influence, the Southerners had only broadened the hope and intensified the determination of Northerners to re-make the South.

TWO

Reconstruction
without Regeneration
1860s—1870s

WITH THE CIVIL WAR CAME A HEAVEN-SENT OPPORTUNITY
to Northernize the South, or so it seemed to those who
desired to do just that. At the war's end most of them
were confident that the victory itself, together with the
prospect of abolition, would suffice to accomplish their
purpose. Soon the conviction spread that further steps
would be necessary—at the least, a fairly large-scale
movement of Northern men and money to the South;
at the most, the confiscation and redistribution of the
planters' lands.

A favorite word of the Northernizers, now as before,
was *regeneration*. They talked of "regenerating" the South
during and after the Civil War in much the same way
that Americans had talked of regenerating Mexico during and after the Mexican War. But Southerners grew
more rather than less resistant to Yankeefication as a
result of their defeat, the loss of their slaves, the arrival
of settlers and capital from the North, and finally the
radical reorganization of their states. The nation was
reconstructed, but the South was not regenerated.

At the start of the Civil War a majority of Northerners, Republicans as well as Democrats, agreed that their only aim was to restore the Union. The war was *not* "'against the South,' or against Southern institutions," insisted the *New York Times*, a thoroughly pro-Lincoln paper. The "loyal people of the Free States," the *Times* went on to explain, were fighting against treason and not against a section. "What they demand of the seceding States is, not that they shall change their domestic institutions, their Constitutions, their policy or their laws, but that they shall return to their allegiance to the Government." Once the seceding states had come back, they would have "all their rights unimpaired," all their institutions "subject to their own control."[1]

But antislavery Republicans began to wonder whether it would be possible to restore and maintain the Union without remodeling the South. Not only the well-known abolitionist William Lloyd Garrison but also the former Democrat and conservative Orestes A. Brownson promptly raised this question, and Brownson reported that "large numbers" who previously had "had no sympathy with Abolitionists" were doing the same. "However homogeneous in race or character, habits or manners, may be the people of a country in the outset," Brownson wrote, "they separate, and grow gradually into two distinct peoples, with almost entirely different ideas, habits and customs, if one half of them in the one section adopt the Slave System, and the other half in the other the Free-Labor System."

Thus, Brownson continued, Americans had "grown almost into two distinct nations." Although the Confederates no longer retained the "original American character," the Northerners were still essentially "the same people that made the Revolution, won American Independence, and established the Federal government." The

only way to recover "the unity and homogeneousness of
the whole American people"—the only way to have one
nation permanently—was to impose upon the South the
labor system of the North. Fortunately, "the Slave States,
by their unprovoked rebellion," had given Northerners
a chance to homogenize and unify the country while
"performing an act of long delayed justice to the negro
population."[2]

Oliver Wendell Holmes made another strong case for
reunion through emancipation when, on July 4, 1863,
he addressed his fellow Bostonians on the causes of the
war. Holmes told his audience that the "antagonism of
the two sections" had resulted from a "movement in mass
of two different forms of civilization in different directions." Alexis de Tocqueville, he recalled, had foreseen
that "the Union was to be endangered by slavery, not
through its interests, but through the change of character it was bringing about in the people of the two sections, the same fatal change which George Mason, more
than half a century before, had declared to be the most
pernicious effect of the system, adding the solemn warning, now fearfully justifying itself" in the ongoing blood-
shed.[3]

Holmes's reasoning dictated that there could be no
lasting peace or union so long as Southern character
remained fundamentally different from Northern. As
Francis Parkman put the matter to Bostonians on another occasion, "It was a strange union that linked us to
the South, and one that can never be renewed until we
have thrust regeneration, total and absolute, into the
innermost being of our adversary."[4]

President Lincoln did not entirely share the feelings
or the aims of radicals such as Garrison, Brownson,
Holmes, and Parkman when he rather tardily proceeded against slavery by proclaiming emancipation and
by urging the Thirteenth Amendment. Lincoln seems

to have had reunion but not regeneration in mind. Even so, he went much too far to please most Democrats. They generally avoided or resisted any suggestion of making it a war aim to reform Southern society in any respect.

The conspicuous Peace Democrat Clement L. Vallandigham insisted in 1863 that New England rather than the South should be remade—and would be. According to this Copperhead, who boasted of his Southern blood, New Englanders a generation earlier had seized upon the slavery question as a political stratagem "to separate the West from the South, and bind her wholly to the North." But the antagonism between New England and the South was not basically one between "slave-holding and non-slaveholding sections." It was, instead, "the old conflict of the Cavalier and the Roundhead, the Liberalist and the Puritan," the "Southron" and the Yankee.

To Vallandigham, as earlier to Daniel R. Hundley, *Yankee* did not signify all Northerners or even all New Englanders. "In many parts of the Northwest—I might add of Pennsylvania, New Jersey, and New York city—the prejudice against the 'Yankee' has always been almost as bitter as in the South," Vallandigham said. In New England there was "really a very large and most liberal and conservative non-Puritan element" which had once been able to check the "narrow, presumptuous, and fanatical spirit of the old Puritan element," before this latter element caused abolitionism to "overspread the whole of New England first, and then the middle States, and finally every State in the Northwest." At last, as Vallandigham saw it, all the anti-Yankee forces were about to unite, and the West, preferring peace to an abolitionist crusade, was about to rejoin the South.[5]

Not all Northern Democrats took the same stand as Vallandigham, though he succeeded in writing into their 1864 platform his demand for a prompt ceasefire. But apparently most of them agreed with him in opposing a war of "aggression, conquest, and revolution" and approving only a war for reunion. As the New Englander and former Whig Robert C. Winthrop put it, "We are not for wading through seas of blood in order to reorganize the whole social structure of the South."[6] In any event, the majority of Northern voters seemingly rejected the Democratic platform and endorsed the Republican, with its plank for an antislavery amendment, when they reelected Lincoln in 1864.

According to Radical Republicans, the war aims included not only the emancipation of the poor blacks but also the liberation of the poor whites—the old objective of North Carolina's Hinton Rowan Helper. Some 300,000 slaveholders, Wendell Phillips said, had been "befooling the seven million of poor whites into being their tools," and "this order of nobles, this privileged class," had "been able for forty years to keep the Government in dread." When used by Phillips, and by many other Republicans, the term *poor whites* referred to all non-slaveholders in the South. Republicans saw these people as potential friends. "The danger of slavery has always been in the poor whites," James Russell Lowell declared, " . . . and the deadliest enemies of slavery will be found among those who have suffered most from its indirect evils."

Thus, in the view of men like Phillips and Lowell, it was a war of democracy against aristocracy, of democracy against despotism. "Such a war," Phillips averred, "finds no parallel nearer than that of the Catholic and the Huguenot of France, or that of the Aristocrat and Republican in 1790, or of Cromwell and the Irish, when victory meant extermination." But to Phillips victory meant the extermination of the Southern system, not of the Southern people. Once both the war and slavery had come to an end, the Negroes would be bound to the Union by "the indissoluble tie of gratitude" and the whites

by "prosperity," as they were "all lifted in the scale of
civilization and activity, educated and enriched. Our institutions are then homogeneous."

Lowell was equally optimistic about the results of abolition. "That extinction accomplished, our wounds will
not be long in healing," he believed. "Apart from the
slaveholding class, which is numerically small, and would
be socially insignificant without its privileges, there are
no such mutual antipathies between the two sections as
the conspirators, to suit their own purposes, have asserted, and even done their best to excite." It was foolish,
Lowell thought, to "talk of the South as our future Poland," though the "stability of peace" would have to be
assured. With peace restored and slavery "rooted out,"
sectional harmony would be "sure to follow."

Speculating on the consequences of the war, Lowell
wrote after three years of it: "One of its more immediate
results has already been to disabuse the Southern mind
of some of its most fatal misconceptions as to Northern
character." Southerners would never again make the
mistake of regarding Northerners as a mere "trading
people" who were "ready to sacrifice everything for
commercial advantage,—a heterogeneous rabble, fit only
to be ruled by a superior race." The North was now "a
great country united in one hope, inspired by one
thought, and welded into one power" through the war's
effects.

"But have not the same influences produced the same
results in the South, and created there also a nation
hopelessly alien and hostile?" Not quite, it seemed to
Lowell. With the destruction of slavery the rebels would
give in, and the war would result "in making us the most
powerful and prosperous community the world ever saw.
Our example and our ideas will react more powerfully
than ever on the Old World, and the consequences of a

rebellion, aimed at [i.e., against] the natural equality of all men, will be to hasten incalculably the progress of equalization over the whole earth." From this grand future the rebels would not necessarily be excluded: "The high qualities they have undoubtedly shown in the course of the war, their tenacity, patience, and discipline, show that, under better influences, they may become worthy to take their part in advancing the true destinies of America."[7]

Another poet, Walt Whitman, had a vision similar to Lowell's. By virtue of "the Secession War and its results," Whitman commented at its end, the United States was now ready to enter upon its "genuine career in history" as a "great Homogeneous Nation,—Free States all—a moral and political unity in variety." The South had "escaped as from the pressure of a general nightmare" and, "notwithstanding all the Southern vexations and humiliations of the hour," was going to participate fully in the great national development of the future. "And I predict," said Whitman, "that the South is yet to outstrip the North."[8]

The famed abolitionist William Lloyd Garrison was one of the most enthusiastic in describing the kind of future the war was about to bring. "Oh . . . how it delights my heart when I think that the worst thing we propose to do for the South is the very best thing that God or man can do!" Thus Garrison had declaimed at a Fourth of July picnic during the first year of the war. "Yes, we will make it possible for them to be a happy and prosperous people, as they never have been, and never can be, with slavery. We will make it possible for them to have free schools, and free presses, and free institutions, as we do at the North." When the Thirteenth Amendment went into effect, in December 1865, Garrison was satisfied that his work was done. "Hail, redeemed, re-

generated America!" he wrote in the next-to-last issue
of his paper, *The Liberator*. "Hail, the Future, with its
pregnant hopes, its glorious promises, its illimitable
powers of expansion and development!"[9]

So the war had been won and slavery had been abolished. The South and the North were now to be not only
harmonious but homogeneous. The new nation, unified
and assimilated, was to enter a period of unexampled
progress, prosperity, greatness, and glory, and the South
was likely to do even better than the North. The American people were increasingly to enjoy the benefits of
equality and opportunity as these spread in ever widen-
ing circles throughout the nation and the world. To those
who believed all this, it seemed that Southerners ought
to be fully as happy as Northerners at the war's outcome—or even happier.

➤➤✕◄◄

In fact, of course, the war only intensified the anti-Yankee
bitterness of Southerners and made them, on the whole,
less willing than ever to accept and adopt Northern ways.
They, too, believed that civilization was at stake—but they
saw themselves as its defenders. "Our cause is holy—
theirs hellish," Confederate Captain Matthew Fontaine
Maury declared at the outset, no doubt expressing the
feelings of most people in the Confederacy. "We want
nothing of the North. We choose not to submit to Northern domination; we are fighting simply to be let alone."[10]

In the South the term *Yankee*, referring to all who supported the Lincoln war, now acquired connotations even
more venomous than it had had in antebellum days. The
word sometimes occasioned humor, but humor that left
a rather bitter aftertaste.

This the diary-keeping Mary Boykin Chesnut of South

Carolina illustrated with a couple of anecdotes. "Mrs. McLean was very angry with [Jefferson Davis's nephew] Joe Davis: he forgot her presence and wished all Yankees were dead. Somebody said he did remember ladies' presence, for the habit of our men was to call them 'Damn Yankees.' . . . And then somebody told a story—a little girl came running to tell on her brother: 'Oh, mama, Charlie is using bad language—curse words.' 'What is it?' 'He says "Damn Yankees" are here prisoners.' [Charlie protested:] 'Well, mama, is not that their name? I never heard them called anything else.'"[11]

Another diarist, Catherine Ann Devereux Edmondston of North Carolina, recorded a story on the same theme:

Sue told me so laughable an instance of the detestation of Yankees in even little children that I cannot let it pass. Little Laura, the youngest but one of brother's children, a saucy little four year old, being out of temper generally & desiring to make an exhibition of it, began thus: "I loves *Rats*, I does! I loves spiders, I does." No notice being taken of her ill humour, she rose higher on the scale of antipathies— "I loves Thousands (ie. thousand legs—centipedes) I does! I say, I loves lizzards, I does! I loves snakes too, I does. Sister Nan do you hear me? I say, I loves *Yankees*, I does," which was as far as she could go! Talk of reunion with a nation classed in the minds of little ones such as this with "*Rats, Thousand Legs, & Snakes.*"

But, for Mrs. Edmondston, the subject was seldom a laughing matter. The expression "Damn Yankee" was far too mild for her, and it became less and less adequate as the war went on. From time to time she referred to "these vile, leveling Yankees," these "mean," "miserable," "loathed," "wily" Yankees, these "mercenary Yankee knaves." She had more than her fill of "Yankee wickedness and meanness," of Yankee "impertinence," "effrontery," "barbarity," "bravado," and "bragg," of Yankee "fiends," "tricks," and "lies." "We no longer will hold any intercourse with you, ye puritanical deceitful race, ye descendants of the Pilgrims, of the hypocrites who came over in the Mayflower," Mrs. Edmondston wrote after only a year of war. "Plume yourselves on your *piety*, your civilization. Wrap yourselves in your own fancied superiority. We are none of you, desire naught from you. We detest you!" And after four years, in defeat, she inwardly raged while she outwardly conformed to the demands of the conquering Yankees. She would swear allegiance to the United States if she had to, but she would not consider the oath binding and would, silently for the time being, continue to detest. "Yes Yankee nation, 'cute' as you are, you cannot fathom the depth of hate, contempt, & rage with which you have filled the breast of every true Southron." [12]

At about the same time another diary-keeping Southerner, the Virginian Edmund Ruffin, left an even more awesome curse. "I here declare my unmitigated hatred to Yankee rule—to all political, social and business connections with the Yankees and to the Yankee race. Would that I could impress these sentiments, in their full force, on every living Southerner and bequeath them to every one yet to be born! May such sentiments be held universally in the outraged and down-trodden South, though in silence and stillness, until the now far-distant day shall arrive for just retribution for Yankee usurpation, oppression and atrocious outrages, and for deliverance and vengeance for the now ruined, subjugated and enslaved Southern States!" [13] Having written those words, Ruffin put the muzzle of a shotgun in his mouth and, with a forked stick, pushed the trigger.

Howell Cobb, recently a general in the Confederate army, soon to be a lawyer in Macon, Georgia, pondered ways that the "bitter animosities" could be "softened" and a "devastated country restored." It would require a great deal of "magnanimity and generosity" on the part

of the conquerors, he thought. "The prejudices and passions which have been aroused in this contest, crimsoned
in the blood of loved ones from every portion of the
land, will yield only to the mellowing influences of time,
and the youngest participant in the struggle will scarcely
live to see the last shadow pass away." But even time
would have its healing effect, in Cobb's opinion, only if
the federal government should properly restrain itself.
The abolition of slavery was "calculated to excite the
most serious apprehensions" and was "unfortunate" for
both whites and blacks. The task of statesmanship now
was to find a "substitute" for slavery. "I take it for granted,"
Cobb said, "that the future relations between the negroes and their former owners, like all other questions
of domestic policy, will be under the control and direction of the State Governments."[14]

Recent Confederates were relieved and Radical Republicans exasperated when President Andrew Johnson made
arrangements for the quick restoration of the seceded
states. The Republicans countered by excluding them
from representation in Congress, and for nearly three
years (1865–68) those governments remained in a kind
of limbo. As time passed, the Radicals became less and
less convinced that surrender and abolition would be
enough, and they gave more and more attention to additional measures for achieving their fundamental objective.

That objective the Radical spokesmen now reaffirmed
and reemphasized. "It is intended," Congressman Thaddeus Stevens of Pennsylvania frankly stated in 1865, with
reference to the Southerners, "to revolutionize their
principles and feelings . . . [to] work a radical reorgani-

zation in Southern institutions, habits, and manners."
Wendell Phillips said the former Confederate states
should not be readmitted to the Union until the North
had succeeded in making the South over "in its likeness."
James Russell Lowell had his Yankee philosopher-farmer
Hosea Biglow tell in verse what to do with the Southern
people:

> Make 'em Amerikin, an' they'll begin
> To love their country ez they loved their sin;
> Let 'em stay Southun, an' you've kep' a sore
> Ready to fester ez it done afore.[15]

If Congress should accept the states that Johnson had
"restored," it could not constitutionally impose on them,
as more or less sovereign entities, the drastic program
that the case required. On this the Radical leaders agreed.
They must treat the South as mere federal territory in
order to rehabilitate the rebels. "This can only be done
by treating and holding them as a conquered people,"
Stevens explained.[16] He reasoned that through defeat in
war the Confederacy had been reduced to a collection
of "conquered provinces" and hence to a territorial sta-
tus. Senator Charles Sumner of Massachusetts arrived
at the same conclusion by a different line of reasoning.
Through the act of seceding, Sumner argued, the
Southern states had committed suicide and had thus re-
verted to territories.

The program that Sumner and Stevens had in mind
involved confiscation. They proposed to take large plantations from the ex-rebel owners and to divide the land
among freed blacks, landless Southern whites, and veterans of the Union army. Sumner had seen this as a
prospect when, in 1862, Congress was considering the
bill that became the Second Confiscation Act. He had
prophesied at that time: "Brave soldiers who have left
their Northern skies to fight the battles of their country,

resting at last from their victories, and changing their
swords into ploughshares, will fill the land with Northern industry and Northern principles."[17] Stevens continued to demand farms for freedmen, while Sumner turned
to advocating suffrage for them. At the end of the war,
however, the federal government held comparatively little
confiscated real estate and it was soon to give back most
of what it held. Congress was never to enact the thor-
oughgoing kind of confiscatory law that Stevens repeatedly called for.

Nevertheless, the prospects for redistribution and re-
settlement of Southern land grew bright for interested
Northerners as the war drew to a close. The land would
be divided, if not by confiscation, then by the operation
of economic laws, the Massachusetts businessman Edward Atkinson wrote confidently in the *North American
Review* in 1864. The "whole cotton country must be per-
meated and regenerated by New England men and New
England ideas," he urged. Already, he noted, emanci-
pated slaves were cultivating abandoned lands along the
Mississippi River and on the South Carolina coast.
Hundreds of Northerners, many of them "substantial
New England men," were preparing to lease other abandoned plantations from the War Department, in the en-
thusiastic belief that "no such opening for enterprise
and capital was ever before offered in this country."
Freedmen's aid societies were sending teachers from the
North to educate the black children.

"Then picture this land as it shall surely be a few years
hence," Atkinson rhapsodized, " . . . the freedmen developing, as at Port Royal, the desire to become land-
owners, and enabled to become so by the large profits
which the next few years must yield to all cultivators of
cotton,—villages established,—the Yankee school-teacher

everywhere at work,—the men in the fields,—the women in their new homes,—the children at school,—none clad now in coarse hand-made fabrics, but in New England manufactures purchased and paid for with their own money,—the poor white trash no longer repelled and forced to spread over Southern Illinois and Indiana the darkness of Egypt, but at home slowly and surely learning . . . true independence."[18]

A year later, after Appomattox, a New Yorker writing in the *Merchants' Magazine* reemphasized migration from the North and from abroad as the means by which the South was to be *"regenerated."* "The large addition that will almost immediately be made to the population of each of those States by citizens from the non-slaveholding States and by emigrants from the various countries of Europe," Charles P. Kirkland predicted, "will subserve a highly useful purpose in the great matter of the 'reconstruction of society,'" ending forever the old aristocratic order.[19]

Among those who expected to invigorate the South— and to get rich while doing so—were Union officers and soldiers. Though they numbered tens of thousands, these men were nevertheless somewhat exceptional, for the great majority of the Boys in Blue who served in the South had no use for that part of the country and no desire to remain or return there. If they did anything to make the Southern people similar to themselves, they did it inadvertently, even though afterward Ralph Waldo Emerson thought they had done a great deal. "The armies mustered in the North were as much missionaries to the mind of the country as they were carriers of material force, and had the vast advantage of carrying whither they marched a higher civilization," Emerson said in dedicating a Massachusetts soldiers' monument.

"The invasion of Northern farmers, mechanics, engineers, tradesmen, lawyers and students did more than forty years of peace had done to educate the South."[20]

But the wartime invasion had not done enough, and quite a few veterans suspected that a peacetime invasion would be necessary. Fairly typical of them was a soldier, about to be mustered out in Texas, who told his sister back home in Ohio that he and some of his comrades were thinking of staying on. John A. Gillis wrote: "Men with Northern hands and brains are in demand here and all over the South, and they will inaugurate a revolution in the condition of the South." Significantly, this man was no Reconstruction radical. "I do hope the question of the nigger may soon be settled," he added, "but I for one am opposed to allowing negroes to vote."[21]

General William Tecumseh Sherman also opposed Negro suffrage, as well as confiscation and other radical measures, and he believed that Union veterans by themselves could transform the South and elevate its civilization. "Young men, such as you, have gone south. I found Memphis and Arkansas full of them. You can work negroes with good profit to yourself and good results to the country." So wrote Sherman, several months after the war's end, to Willard Warner, a young friend and fellow Ohioan. A former Union officer who had taken up cotton planting in Alabama, Warner would later become a Republican senator from that state. "We now have the power to transform that vast area heretofore kept in a low state of civilization by causes for which this generation was not responsible, to the very highest, by education, by industry, by patience, by forbearance and the simple practice of that charity which is the foundation of religion and wisdom," Sherman elaborated. "Congress can't do it by all the test oaths and voluminous trammelings of statutes, but the young men of this country can and will."[22]

"Go West, young man," the slogan once had been; now it was also "Go South." The "openings which the South presents for Northern capital and industry are unsurpassed," the journalist Whitelaw Reid discovered during his Southern travels of 1865–66. These opportunities are at least "as attractive as those that are drawing emigration into the uninhabited wilds across the Rocky Mountains." In the South "a Northern farmer, devoting himself to cotton-growing, may count with safety on a net profit of fifty per cent on his investment." The Northerner could also do handsomely at producing sugar, lumbering the pine and cypress forests, or engaging in a profession or trade. Tens of thousands, many if not most of them Union veterans, responded to the lure. The wandering reporter John T. Trowbridge heard that, by January 1866, there were at least fifty thousand Northerners in Louisiana alone.

As early as September 1865 a roving correspondent of the *Boston Advertiser*, Sidney Andrews, had found "many Northern men" already in Charleston, South Carolina. The "various 'Northern houses' . . . appeared to include at least half of the stores on each side of the principal streets." These merchants brought "Yankee notions"— "notions" in the double sense of goods and beliefs. "To bring here the conveniences and comforts of our Northern civilization, no less than the Northern idea of right and wrong, justice and injustice, humanity and inhumanity," Andrews commented, "is the work ready for the hand of every New England man and woman who stands waiting." To Andrews the Northerners in the South (at least those in Charleston) appeared to be missionaries as well as merchandisers.

Some Northern observers, however, developed quite
a different impression. In New Orleans and elsewhere
Whitelaw Reid was disgusted to see Northerners conforming to Southern prejudice. "This flunkeyism of
Northern men, who 'expected to stay in this country and
didn't want to make enemies,' was manifest everywhere,"
Reid reported. "If they were found out to be Northerners, they were anxious to have it understood that, at any
rate, they were not Yankees." In an editorial on "Dry-
Goods Drummers at the South," *Harper's Weekly* went even
further in denouncing "the men who go among them,
and who, in order to secure their custom, outdo rebels
themselves in their expression of rebel sentiments. In
fact, it must be admitted that now, as before the war, the
class of Northern men who go Southward, seeking custom, or designing to make a permanent stay, are the
most despicable representatives of the North, and form
the most dangerous class of Southern citizens."

Even allowing for considerable exaggeration in such
reports, it seems evident that comparatively few Northerners made any conscious effort to change Southern
customs or attitudes. In any case, the number of Northerners in the South soon rapidly declined. The "great
rush," as Reid noted, was "already over" by the beginning of 1866. Thereafter migration continued at a lower
rate than before—and for a time at a much lower rate
than the northward movement of returning, disillusioned migrants.[23] Their failure and disillusionment were
due in large part to the reception that Southerners had
given them.

Though mixed, the reception was on the whole un-
friendly—as perhaps the arriving Northerners should

have expected it to be. The less hospitable Southerners insisted that the South retain its separate identity. "The victory over Southern arms is to be followed by a victory over Southern *opinions*," the *Christian Index* of Macon, Georgia, warned. To prevent such an outcome, the Richmond newspaperman Edward A. Pollard called for a "war of ideas" in his book *The Lost Cause* (1866). The Southern people, Pollard counseled, should not be overeager to "bring in Northern capital and labor" and "make themselves rivals in the clattering and garish enterprise of the North," for there were "higher objects than the Yankee *magna bona* of money and display, and loftier aspirations than the civilization of material things." The Southern cause, Pollard implied, was not yet completely lost. "It would be immeasurably the worst consequence of defeat in this war that the South should lose its moral and intellectual distinctiveness as a people, and cease to assert its well-known superiourity [*sic*] in civilization, in political scholarship, and in all the standards of individual character over the people of the North."

Churchmen took up the Lost Cause with particular zeal. Prominent among them was Albert Taylor Bledsoe, a Methodist minister and a former University of Virginia professor, proslavery advocate, and Confederate propagandist. To advance the cause, Bledsoe founded the *Southern Review* in 1867. "The great defect of Northern civilization is its materiality," he wrote therein. "It is of the earth, earthy; and ignores the spirituality of our nature." Defenders of the cause preached that Northern wealth was sinful and Southern poverty a blessing.[24]

Still, a few self-appointed spokesmen for the South welcomed men and money from the North. *De Bow's Review*, which before the war had advocated both industrialization and sectional exclusiveness, afterward championed industrialization and sectional reconciliation. "We all, North, South, East, and West, have *one country, one destiny, one duty,*" James D. B. De Bow proclaimed in January 1866, while inviting immigrants and capital. The South Carolinian James L. Orr, the postwar governor of his state, frankly confessed: "I am tired of South Carolina as she was. I covet for her the material prosperity of New England. I would have her acres teem with life and vigour and intelligence, as do those of Massachusetts." Even Pollard, reversing his stand, soon came out for a "New South," one that would be much like the North. In *The Lost Cause Regained* (1868) he urged Southerners to undertake a "social reconstruction," to emulate the "superior thrift and enterprise" of Northerners, to encourage their immigration and investment, and indeed to adopt all the things he quite recently had condemned as Yankee evils. Thus might the South enter upon "a new era of material prosperity."

Edwin De Leon, another South Carolinian and a former propagandist for the Confederacy, made himself a propagandist, in an 1870 issue of *Putnam's Magazine,* for what he also called "The New South." There "can be no doubt of the rapid fusion of the social and material elements" of the two sections, De Leon averred, for "each successive day blends and binds more intimately together the lives and fortunes of the two, owing to the movement of Northern men and capital southwards." De Leon went on to say, "The Northerner will carry south his thrift, his caution, his restless activity, his love of new things; the Southerner will temper these with his reckless liberality, his careless confidence, his fiery energy, and his old-time conservatism; and both will be benefited by the admixture."[25]

Some reports from the South indicated that Northern influence would, indeed, prevail. General Philip H.

Sheridan, in command of the Military Division of the Gulf, thought so in January 1866. "The Southern country, in the General's opinion, was fast becoming 'Northernized,'" Trowbridge reported after interviewing Sheridan at his New Orleans headquarters. "The planters had no enterprise, no recuperative energy: they were entirely dependent upon Northern capital and Northern spirit." The general must soon have had second thoughts, for less than six months later he told Massachusetts Senator Henry Wilson that the ex-rebels would "chafe and be restless for a long time" not only because of their defeat and their property losses but also because of their "fear of being absorbed by emigrants and capital from the United States." Still, the Scotsman David Macrae, after his Southern trip of 1867–68, concluded that, with "Yankee and foreign enterprise" coming in, the Southern people were noticeably changing. "The change seemed to be summed up in an expression which met me constantly in the South—'Yes, sir, we are getting Yankeeized.'"[26]

According to the reports, the response of the Southern people was far from uniform; it varied, for one thing, with social class. "The leading men generally invite immigration, and are honest and sincere in their expression of desire for the influx of new life," Andrews concluded after his 1865 tour of Georgia and the Carolinas, "but the masses of the people have little disposition of welcome for Northerners." Moreover, the fact "that any opinion savors of the 'Yankee'—in other words, is new to the South—is a fact that even prevents its consideration by the great body of the people. Their inherent antagonism to everything from the North—an antagonism fostered and cunningly cultured for half a century by the politicians in the interest of slavery—is something that no traveller can photograph, that no Northern man can understand, till he sees it with his own eyes, hears it with his own ears, and feels it by his own consciousness."

In 1866 Trowbridge found in South Carolina a "virulent animosity existing in the minds of the common people, against the government and people of the North," but he also found a "class of men" who showed "courteous hospitality and liberal views. Instead of insulting and repelling Northern men, they invite them, and seem eager to learn of them the secret of Northern enterprise and prosperity." John R. Dennett, a writer for the New York weekly *The Nation*, heard from a former Union army officer who was practicing law in New Orleans: "Yes, I believe that all the men of wealth and influence and integrity, the solid men, are disposed to be loyal, and to behave like good citizens." It was the "brawlers in bar-rooms and billiard saloons" who were "always damning the Yankees."[27]

That same year the *Chicago Tribune* published a letter from an army officer who had been recently stationed in Alabama: "The facts are that in Alabama there is a class of men, intelligent and usually wealthy, . . . who certainly desire Northern men to come in among them with their capital, to engage in planting, trading, manufacturing, &c. But the majority of the people are still very bitter and opposed to Northern men coming into the State." And in 1867 the *Philadelphia Press* editorialized: "No doubt the substantial portion of the community South desire to invite moneyed and industrial immigration, but there is a class of irresponsible young men who generally manage to speak for and overawe the entire population."[28]

If these reports are to be believed (and certainly they tend to confirm one another), the ex-Rebels least hostile to incoming Northerners and least resistant to Northern influence were to be found among the comparatively

well to do—that is, among the former slaveowners. The
most hostile were the white masses, the so-called (and
miscalled) poor whites, the farmers who had never been
able to afford a slave. Here was an irony that none of the
reporters noticed. Before and during the war, Republicans had assumed that the slaveholding planters were
their abiding enemies, and the non-slaveholding farmers their potential friends. Presumably these common
people, suffering from the oppression of the aristocrats,
would be grateful to their Northern liberators and glad
to adopt a Northern point of view. But now, after the
war, it appeared that the positions of planter and poor
white were practically the reverse of what had been anticipated.

According to Northern observers, the attitudes of
Southerners varied not only with social class but also
with time, place, and other factors. There seemed to be
the most anti-Yankee feeling in South Carolina, and the
least in North Carolina. Towns, especially large ones along
frequented routes of travel, were less inhospitable than
isolated rural areas. On the whole, women were more
defiant than men, and male stay-at-homes more hostile
than Confederate veterans. As the months passed, however, larger and larger numbers of all these groups, even
of the recent soldiers, showed signs of animosity toward
Northerners in the South. "For some time after the 'Surrender,'" an army officer on duty in Arkansas wrote just
one year after Appomattox, "those who had returned
from the Rebel armies were the most quiet and orderly.
It is not so now."

Even those Southerners who favored "an influx of
Northern energy and Northern capital," as Andrews reported, did not necessarily welcome an influx of Northern principles and prejudices. A man from Columbus,
Georgia, was pleased enough to see the southward mi-

gration. "Yet when the Yankees come down here," he
insisted, "they'll have to be Georgians if they reckon to
make money." An increasing majority of Southerners
were unwilling to accept Northerners on any terms. More
and more the natives greeted the newcomers with in-
sults, boycotts, threats, and actual violence. "Why is it
that immigration and investment force their way through
the passes of the Rocky Mountains rather than enter the
inviting fields of the South?" the *Philadelphia Press* asked
late in 1867, after most of the postwar migrants from
the North had returned home. "The answer is simple.
It is not safe nor pleasant for Northern men to go into
the Southern States to live."[29]

Ill will met not only Northern men—aspiring planters, merchants, lawyers, and the like—but also Northern
women, the schoolteachers who went south to educate
the children of the recent slaves. "The rebels' great bug-
bear now is the Northern school-ma'm," the Charleston
correspondent of the *Chicago Tribune* reported in 1867.
"She occupies the same position in their minds . . . that
John Brown and the Abolitionists did previous to the
war." Whites feared that the teachers would convert the
blacks into Yankees. Indeed, the teachers aspired to do
essentially that, although they encountered frustration
and disappointment. In Georgia the freed people generally clung to their traditional values and rejected the
Puritan virtues that the educational missionaries tried to
instill. Like Southern whites, but in their own way,
Southern blacks resisted Yankeefication.[30]

The growing bitterness of Southern whites reflected
"the course of events at Washington"—the prolonged
exclusion of the Southern states from representation in
Congress, the passage of the Civil Rights Bill and the
Freedmen's Bureau Bill over President Johnson's veto,
and the preparation of a Fourteenth Amendment to the

Constitution. "To all this was added . . . the seeming desire to force upon the Southern people the political and social equality of the freed men," a Louisianian complained to Senator John Sherman of Ohio. "Is it wise that these States should feel that they are no better off than Poland or Hungary!" he continued. "Will not the hatred which harsh words and arbitrary measures beget be handed down to future generations, and may they not produce fruit when these fertile and now free States count their inhabitants as do New York and Ohio by millions?"

General Sherman endorsed and sent on to Senator Sherman a letter from Willard Warner, the Shermans' Ohio friend in Alabama, urging the prompt readmittance of the Southern states. "It is not wise, nor have we the just right," Warner had written, "to force on them schemes of reform, more or less Utopian in their character, & which we ourselves—the Northern people—have not accepted." An Ohioan in New Orleans, L. A. Sheldon, wrote to Congressman James A. Garfield: "My opinion is that hostility will die sooner by restoring the states than by the continued exclusion." The *Merchants' Magazine* argued for their early restoration on the grounds that this would end disorder and thus make it possible for Northerners to "develope the wealth of the South."[31]

Warner and Sheldon conceded that there were risks for some Northerners in the return of Southerners to national politics. Warner expected the South to "stand with the West" and against the East "on questions of the tariff." Sheldon said of the Southerners: "They . . . hope to be able to strike hands with the Northwest and overcome the influence of New England. They affect to like us [Ohioans and other Westerners] and to be ready to harmonize at once. They are willing to admit that we whipped them out, but [they insist] that New England did not and cannot." Still another Ohioan, General Robert K. Scott, the head of the South Carolina Freedmen's Bureau, held a somewhat similar view. "The South will do by Diplomacy what they failed to do by the Sword," Scott predicted. "They will try what a je[a]lousy between the East and West will accomplish first."[32] Here were intimations of a sectionalism dividing the North and hindering the Northernization of the South, sectionalism of the kind that Clement L. Vallandigham had expressed in the Thirty-seventh Congress and William Maclay had augured in the First.

Scott opposed a quick reopening of national politics to Southern whites. He saw them as "a set of Educated Barbarians" with a murderous hatred for "smart Negroes," or for that matter any Negroes who had "the *Insolence* to assert their *Rights*." A Maine man residing in North Carolina agreed essentially with Scott. "The Southern people are in the main a cheap and ignorant set, and much addicted to *intoxication*," G. F. Granger wrote to Thaddeus Stevens; "to see a Southern politician *sober* is an anomaly. As far as meanness trickery and Yankee sharpness go I can safely say they out Herod Herod." If the Southern states should soon be restored, they would be unsafe for Northerners to reside or invest in: "In short, I firmly believe that nothing but military power of the Gov'm't . . . will make the South safe for Northern Industry and Capital . . . without this military protection the South will be as much shut up to the North, as Japan or China used to be."

Thus, in the minds of some Northerners, military reconstruction, which was soon to come, was an instrument of both economic and cultural imperialism. It was also a means of confirming the recent victory, of guaranteeing freedom to the former slaves and making re-

union and democracy secure. Albion W. Tourgée, a war
veteran from Ohio who had made his postwar home in
North Carolina, put the case emphatically in speeches
he gave on a Northern tour in the fall of 1866. Tourgée
was campaigning against the Johnson policy and in favor
of radical reconstruction with suffrage for Southern
blacks. "Southern pride and exclusiveness the basis of
Rebellion," read the notes he spoke from. "South saved
when desouthernized and thoroughly nationalized."[33]

→→)(←←

Northern men residing in the South received a new opportunity to remake its society and culture as well as its
polity—or thought they did—when Congress repassed,
over President Johnson's veto, the Reconstruction Act of
March 1867. This legislation took political rights from
former Confederates (the leaders) and gave them to former slaves. Now, for the first time, the Republican party
could organize in the South. It could expect the support
of nearly all the blacks; it could also appeal to disaffected
Southern whites, especially the old Unionists of 1860–
1861. And it could provide opportunities for the Northerners, who could aspire to positions of leadership that
ex-Confederates previously had held.

Under the Reconstruction Act the Southern states were
to formulate new constitutions while the army tempo-
rarily occupied and controlled the South. When constitutional conventions met in the ten states to be
reconstructed, Northern whites accounted for fewer than
150 of the more than 1,000 delegates. Blacks numbered
about 250, and all the rest were Southern whites. Yet the
Northerners exerted an influence far out of proportion
to their numbers. They collected constitutions from the
Northern states, picked out provisions they liked, and

put these into the constitutions they helped to write for
the Southern states. These provisions gave every man
the right to vote and hold office, made most offices elec-
tive, based representation on population, enlarged the
bills of rights, restricted the death penalty, exempted
homes from seizure for debt, and required the establish-
ment of public schools. Constitutionally, at least, the
Southern states now became more democratic, more
progressive, more Northern than they had ever been
before.[34]

The Union veteran Tourgée, the most influential
member of the North Carolina convention, saw his task
as a delegate to be the championing of "innovation"
against the "customs habits and laws of the good old
times" that conservative Carolinians harked back to. To
him, the new constitution-making had the same essential
purpose as the Union's recent warmaking. "The war from
which we have just emerged," he told the convention,
"was a struggle between Republicanism and Oligarchy,
between the rights of the people and the usurpations of
Aristocracy, between the elevation of the masses and the
exaltation of the few, between feudal theory and free
principles." As a North Carolina judge and a codifier of
the state's laws, he kept on with the struggle. He did
much to simplify procedures and to modernize the legal
system, bringing North Carolina up to the standard of
the most advanced Northern states.

In the reorganized governments Republicans from the
North undertook state action to encourage immigration, promote railroads, establish schools, and in every
possible way bring the South up to date. Providence had
"richly endowed" Arkansas, for example, according to
the incoming governor, the Pennsylvania-born Powell
Clayton, who had settled in Kansas and then had gone
south with the Union army. "Yet, in the midst of this

great age of progress and improvements, our primeval forests, as of yore, rear their fertile arms to Heaven and seem to defy the hand of man," Governor Clayton said in his 1868 inaugural. "We should invite all classes to come here and we should greet everyone with a cordial welcome."

In Congress, once members from the reorganized states had been admitted, those of Northern origin sought the federal government's help in stimulating the economic progress of the South. "The South now needs your aid," Willard Warner of Alabama told his Senate colleagues. "Dig out her harbors; give her the share of bank circulation which belongs to her; aid to build her railroads, and in every way by your practical legislation aid to build up her material interests . . . and . . . you will have done a wise work in the matter of the reconstruction of these States."[35]

Here and there outside observers noted visible evidences of persisting and growing Northern influence in the South, but these signs seemed exceptional rather than typical. A correspondent of the *Boston Traveller* reported that, along the road he took through Virginia in 1869, the few farms "cultivated by the industry and skill of Yankees" were neater and more productive than the many "not cultivated but neglected by the native owners." In 1870 the Englishman Robert Somers, once pro-Confederate, now anti-Radical, found Atlanta booming, its stores "full of 'Northern notions,'" most of its business in the hands of "aspiring Northern men." But Somers also observed: "Many of these enterprising men have already come to grief and left the country, while others are in full career to Fortune, or—her eldest daughter—Miss Fortune."

Edward King, writing for *Scribner's Magazine* in 1874, commented on the potential of Arkansas and the "hand-

some development" of Little Rock, where society and
schools were "as good as in Eastern towns of the same
size. But in the back country!—there the prospect is very
different." Northerners, King saw, had taken over much
of Florida, including the town of Palatka, amid the or-
ange groves they had developed along the St. Johns River.
Whereas "Shooting affrays were common" in the Palatka
of earlier years, "Now the town is as peaceable as moun-
tain resorts in New Hampshire and Vermont." In the
Florida "backwoods," however, one could still find
the ignorance and the "simplicity and boorishness of the
'crackers.'"[36]

Though numerous in certain areas, Southern white
Republicans constituted only a small minority of Southern whites as a whole. As time passed, many went over
to the opposition, and the minority became even smaller.
Southern white Republicans shared the economic vision
of their Northern fellow partisans and repudiated the
anti-Yankee prejudices of the Southern Democrats. "Why
should our agriculture and commerce languish, and our
rivers run idly to the sea? Why have not Northern enterprise and capital poured in upon us?" asked the native
Tar Heel W. W. Holden in 1868. "Under the auspices of
those who involved us in rebellion," continued the man
who would soon be the first Republican governor of his
state, "we are growing poorer every day. These leaders,
instead of inviting immigration, are repelling it by their
sectional counsels, their silly repinings over the unhappy
past, and the narrow-minded, indignant manner in which
they treat those whom they are pleased to term 'Northern adventurers' and 'Radical emissaries.'"

To most white Southerners the imposition of "Negro
rule" (as they liked to call the granting of political rights
to blacks) was the greatest indignity they had yet suffered at the hands of Northerners. The abolitionist threat,

the military conquest, the delayed readmittance—those things had been bad enough. But this latest, this social and political subversion, was far worse. Anti-Yankee feeling now reached new heights in the South.

Ex-Governor Zebulon Vance of North Carolina saw the 1868 campaign against the Republicans as a "struggle for the rights and liberties of our race, for constitutional government and for Christian civilization." A South Carolinian wrote to Thaddeus Stevens, whom Southerners considered the chief author of the Reconstruction Act, to tell him that he, along with all his "aides and political associates," was going to be "put to death." Not a murderer, but a Christian and a patriot would be the man who saved the South from "this awful Yankee despotical sway and rule. Oh how *we, the South,* long for this relief from misrule, military oppression, anarchy and destruction. And all from and by the most cowardly Yankee puritanical devils in this or any other land."[37]

So horrendous, in the view of Southern conservatives, was the Northern Republican in the South that they needed a new epithet for him. The term *Yankee*—with all its evil connotations and even with such modifiers as *awful, cowardly,* and *puritanical*—no longer sufficed. Now, in 1868, Southern along with Northern Democrats began to call the Northern Republican in the South a *carpetbagger.* This word implied that the Yankee had left home with no more possessions than he could carry in a traveling bag, that he aimed to enrich himself in politics by exploiting the Negro vote, and that he was a bird of passage with no lasting interest or stake in the South. And, in the lexicon of conservatives, a Southern white Republican was a "scalawag"—a scoundrelly, low-class, thoroughly obnoxious person, a traitor to his region and his race.[38]

Conservatives blamed the "unprincipled carpetbag-

ger" for race conflict and for "shameful corruption,
bribery and roguery," as Ex-Governor Benjamin F. Perry
blamed Governor Robert K. Scott, the Republican from
Ohio, in South Carolina in 1871. What the *New York Herald* reporter Charles Nordhoff noted in Mississippi in
1875 was true also in other Southern states. "A Northern man, being a Republican, is therefore a 'carpetbagger,' no matter whether he is honest or dishonest," said
Nordhoff, who was no lover of Republicans, white or
black, Northern or native. "His children hear themselves
called 'Yankees' at school, his wife finds her church relations unpleasant. He is looked on with aversion, and
this though he may have brought capital into the State,
may have all his interests there, and have lived there
since the war." Essentially this description fit the so-called
carpetbaggers Tourgée, Clayton, and Warner, and to a
large extent also Scott. As for the scalawags, some were,
as a *Chicago Tribune* correspondent remarked, men of
"property, intelligence, social position."[39]

"The war still exists in a very important phase here,"
it seemed in Mississippi in 1869, at least to the military
governor, Adelbert Ames, a professional soldier from
Maine. Carpetbaggers in other states, too, felt that the
rebellion was continuing or reviving. This time the rebels were going to win. Through the terrorism of the Ku
Klux Klan, the Red Shirts, and other violent organizations, the Democrats or Conservatives soon overthrew
the Republicans in one state after another.

Ames, by then a United States senator from Mississippi, was still keeping up the fight in 1871. "Of the
great benefits and blessings resulting from the crusades
to the Holy Land," he told the Senate, "next in impor-
tance to the dissemination of Christianity were those which
grew out of the intermingling and intercommunion of
the several peoples of Europe. So would great benefits

and blessings result from northern crusades necessitated by the rebellion into benighted regions, were not violence and murder now working their defeat." By 1874, months before his party was to fall to the terrorists in Mississippi, Ames (who was at that time governor of the state) was already in a mood to abandon the crusade. "The North seems the place for us," he wrote to his wife, Blanche, Ben Butler's daughter, in Massachusetts. "Slavery blighted this people—then the war—then reconstruction—all piled on such a basis destroyed the minds—at least impaired their judgement and consciousness to that extent that we cannot live among them."[40]

Daniel H. Chamberlain—a native of Massachusetts, an alumnus of Yale College and the Harvard Law School, and a former officer in the Union army—had to contend with the rifle companies and the armed mobs of the Democrats when he ran for reelection as governor of South Carolina in 1876. When President Rutherford B. Hayes took away the token guard of federal soldiers in 1877, Chamberlain could no longer hold the governor's office, and Radical Reconstruction soon was no more in any Southern state. At the collapse of the Republican regime in Louisiana, a *New York Times* correspondent gave it as his opinion that the "white men from the North" did not need to be ashamed of the term *carpetbagger*, for they had "done much to civilize the South."

After returning to the North, Chamberlain said in a Fourth of July address that Hayes's Southern policy meant the abandonment of the South to "a class whose traditions, principles, and history" were "opposed to every step and feature" of what Republicans considered the "national progress since 1860." Two years later he wrote in the *North American Review* that from 1789 to 1860 the South had been hostile to "all Republican ideas" and that "to-day again, as in 1860, the same oligarchical power" was seeking to "extend and perpetuate its own spirit and practice of caste and oppression."[41]

The best statement of the carpetbagger's conception of what he had been about came from Albion W. Tourgée. In 1879 he decided to leave North Carolina. "I thought I could live in the South," he explained to a *New York Tribune* interviewer. "In 1865 there was less bitterness than now. The rebel soldiers . . . respected their late foes and remembered the earlier days. But since then a new generation has grown up nurtured in hostility." Tourgée's novel *A Fool's Errand* was about to appear. At the end of the story the carpetbag character Colonel Servosse (Tourgée himself) delivers some words of wisdom:

> The North and the South are simply convenient names for two distinct, hostile, and irreconcilable ideas,—two civilizations they are sometimes called, especially at the South. At the North there is somewhat more of intellectual arrogance; and we are apt to speak of the one as civilization, and of the other as a species of barbarism. These two must always be in conflict until the one prevails, and the other falls. To uproot the one, and plant the other in its stead, is not the work of a moment or a day. That was our mistake. We tried to superimpose the civilization, the idea of the North, upon the South at a moment's warning. We presumed that, by the suppression of the rebellion, the Southern white man had become identical with the Caucasian of the North in thought and sentiment; and that the slave, by emancipation, had become a saint and a Solomon at once. So we tried to build up communities there which should be identical in thought, sentiment, growth, and development, with those of the North. It was A FOOL'S ERRAND.[42]

THREE

From New South to No South
1880s–1980s

AFTER FAILING IN RECONSTRUCTION, NORTHERNERS FOR three-quarters of a century made only few and feeble attempts to refashion the South in accordance with their own ideals. Southerners nevertheless continued to discover what they thought were serious threats arising from the North. They felt their worst fears confirmed when, in the 1950s, Northerners began to join the movement to obtain civil rights for Southern blacks. Self-conscious Southerners all along had striven to keep alive a sense of Southern identity, and now they renewed the struggle once again.

It was becoming increasingly difficult, however, to tell the difference, economically or socially, between the South and the rest of the country. The two looked more and more nearly alike as industries and cities grew in the one and the black percentage of the population grew in the other. The South might be "new"—and continually newer—but most of its people insisted that it was still the South. As they had done from the beginning, they defined it in opposition to the North, even though there was no longer much of a contrast. No North, no South. So one might predict, but that would be to underestimate the power of the Southerners' imagination.

By 1879 conditions seemed ripe for the South to make
a fresh start in the direction of the economic progress
that so long had characterized the North. Progress in
the South had been slow and halting because of the political disturbances that accompanied Reconstruction and
because of the nationwide depression that followed the
financial panic of 1873. By the decade's end the state
governments were safely in the hands of conservative
Southern whites, and general prosperity was on the way.
Still, while some of the people looked ahead, others persisted in looking back. During the 1880s and 1890s, as
during the 1870s, the New South had to contend with
the Old.

The loudest and clearest calls for Northernization came
from Southerners themselves. Henry Watterson, editor
of the *Louisville Courier-Journal,* had told a New York City
audience in 1877: "If proselytism be the supreme joy of
mankind, New England must be pre-eminently happy,
for the ambition of the South is to out-Yankee the Yankee." In Mississippi the editor of the *Vicksburg Herald*
wrote in 1881: "We are in favor of the South, from the
Potomac to the Rio Grande, being thoroughly and permanently Yankeeized."[1]

The outstanding journalist of this persuasion was
Henry W. Grady of the *Atlanta Constitution,* and the classic expression of his view was "The New South," the
address he gave at the New England Club of New York
on December 21, 1886. Grady took Abraham Lincoln,
the "first typical American" and the "sum of Puritan and
Cavalier," as the symbol of the merging of Northern and
Southern character. He proceeded to describe and to
boast of the changing South, and in doing so he used
words that in the past had been applied particularly to

the North—words such as "democracy," "schoolhouse," "towns and cities," "industry," "business," "thrift," and "work." Indeed, he attributed to his people—and took great pride in—traits that earlier Southern spokesmen had viewed as typically Yankee and utterly contemptible. "We have let economy take root and spread among us as rank as the crab-grass which sprung from Sherman's cavalry camps, until we are ready to lay odds on the Georgia Yankee as he manufactures relics of the battle-field in a one-story shanty and squeezes pure olive oil out of his cottonseed, against any down-easter that ever swapped wooden nutmegs for flannel sausage in the valleys of Vermont."[2]

But many Southerners, especially churchmen, had serious doubts about the "New South" idea. "All through the South," a Northerner had observed in 1881, "the ministers appear to view 'progress' with a degree of alarm, and certainly with decided reprobation." In an 1882 commencement address at Hampden-Sydney College the Presbyterian theologian Robert Lewis Dabney saw industrialization as inevitable and even desirable, for without it the South would remain "dependent and subordinate," but he prayed that, in industrializing, the South would escape the materialism of the North. Generally the preachers looked upon economic change as a menace to the old-time religion.

A more immediate threat came from the Northern branches of churches that had divided over the slavery question. Northern Methodists and Baptists kept on with their campaign, which they had begun after the war, to reunite and to control their respective organizations. They also continued their missionary work, setting up new congregations in the South. Instead of surrendering, the Southern Methodists and Baptists counterattacked, founding hundreds of churches in the North.

Churches in the South served as bastions against the
incursion not only of Northern religion but of Northern
culture in general. They made the Lost Cause a secular
and even a religious faith. Heading its roster of saints
were the martyred Jefferson Davis and, highest of all,
the Christlike Robert E. Lee. The devil was the North,
whose wartime "barbarities of burning and butchery"
and persisting materialistic and atheistic ways the
preachers allowed none of their congregations to forget.
Auxiliaries of the faith were the nostalgic societies that
took form in the 1890s—the United Confederate Veterans, the United Daughters of the Confederacy, and
the United Sons of the Confederacy. So closely linked
were Christianity and the Lost Cause that one can read-
ily understand the mistake of the little girl who, when
asked if she knew who had crucified her Lord, replied:
"O yes I know, the Yankees."[3]

Outsiders were often struck by the contradictions between the New South and the Old, though one traveler
quickly forgot the old once she had seen the new. Of her
arrival in Richmond in 1883, Lady Duffus Hardy noted:
"Although we are only twelve hours from the booming,
hustling city of New York, yet we feel we have entered a
strange land. The difference is not so much in mere
externals, as that the whole character of life is changed,
and from all sides is borne upon us that we are in the
land of a 'lost cause'; it impregnates the very air we breathe
. . . it reveals itself everywhere and in everything." But
in a day or two, after seeing and hearing of railroads
and factories under way, the English noblewoman declared: "No one visiting the South to-day can recognise
a single feature of its ancient self, so complete is the
change that has swept over the whole land . . . the very
atmosphere seems changed from a sultry enervating air

to an invigorating breeze." The South seemed not so different from the North, after all. "North and south, east and west—all are animated by the same spirit of progress," Lady Duffus Hardy decided.[4]

The Massachusetts-born doctor of divinity Henry M. Field also saw signs of progress when, in 1886, he and several big businessmen took a Southern trip in the private car of the Louisville and Nashville Railroad president. At Charlotte, North Carolina, they left the train to view the countryside, where they were told that large planters had been losing and poor whites gaining in consequence of the war. The Reverend Dr. Field reflected that all this involved a "social change, somewhat like the breaking up of the Feudal System in France." He predicted: "The New South will come when the Carolinas, like Massachusetts and Connecticut, instead of being the territorial appanages of a few families, are divided up into tens of thousands of small farms, cultivated by intelligent, independent, and self-respecting husbandmen." After a stop in Atlanta, Field concluded that, with respect to shops, stores, banks, and schools, Atlanta was "becoming like a Northern city, and Georgia like a Northern State." Addressing a banquet in New Orleans, he invoked the spirit of General Lee in behalf of sectional harmony and economic progress. He also quoted the prophecy that the great Southern orator from Maine, Seargent S. Prentiss, had made in New Orleans forty years earlier—that a time would come when "this Crescent City" should have "filled her golden horns." Then might "the sons of the Pilgrims, still wandering from the bleak hills of the North, stand upon the banks of the Great River, and exclaim, Lo! this is our country!"[5]

After having visited the South in 1867, 1875, and 1887, the Pennsylvania politician and industrialist William D.

("Pig Iron") Kelley had some misgivings about its present but was optimistic about its future. The region, it
seemed to Kelley, "is in a transitional state," and "the
stranger within her borders cannot fail to discover that
he moves in the midst of two communities: one of which
is animated by hope, is full of impulse, enterprise, and
energy, while the other . . . looks only to the past for
inspiration and guidance." There were localities that might
properly be called new. "But apart from the New South,
by which I mean the country around the region of the
rapidly developing iron industries, and of such manufacturing towns as Augusta and Macon, and the commercial centres created by the expansion of the Southern
railroad systems, the same wretched poverty prevails
among the Southern people now, twenty-two years after
the close of the war." The South "must at no distant day
break from the thralldom of a misguided past," Kelley
professed to believe. "She is the coming El Dorado of
American adventure."

Kelley had heard "Southern enthusiasts predict the
speedy transfer to the South of the skill and capital now
engaged in producing iron and steel in Pennsylvania
and Ohio," and he had also heard "Northern pessimists
query as to the time when the cheaper iron of the New
South" would "begin to close the mines and furnaces of
these great iron-producing States." By the 1890s, capital
from the textile industry of Massachusetts also was going
south, and this together with another business depression was closing mills in the cloth-manufacturing cities
of New England. Now that Alabama iron and Carolina
textiles were gaining, the *Philadelphia Times* observed in
1894 that it was beginning to "look as if the Eastern
States would need less protection against European
competition and more against the enterprise of Southern progress."[6]

Wherever and however the South was moving ahead, it was due to an "infusion of Northern blood," the *New York Tribune* had maintained. Lady Duffus Hardy had said, in regard to what she considered the most Northern and most progressive of the Southern states, "The development of Florida has generally been carried on by the northern people." Welcoming the Yankees, Henry W. Grady had assured them in his famous "New South" speech: "We have learned that one Northern immigrant is worth fifty foreigners and have smoothed the path to Southward, wiped out the place where Mason and Dixon's line used to be, and hung out the latch-string to you and yours." But Grady was disappointed in the response to his invitation, and three years later, in 1889, he informed the Boston Merchants' Association at its annual banquet: "The strange fact remains that in 1880 the South had fewer Northern-born citizens than she had in 1870—fewer in '70 than in '60." He blamed this on the "race problem," which in turn he blamed on Reconstruction.[7] Whatever the explanation, there could be no doubt that Northerners, as they had always been, were less willing to move south than Southerners were to move north. The census of 1900 enumerated only 400,000 of the Northern-born living in the South and more than six times as many, about 2,500,000, of the Southern-born living in the North.

Northern residents of the South continued to risk the ill will of native Southerners, though in less violent ways than during Reconstruction. A case in point was Willard Warner, once a Union general from Ohio, later a Republican senator from Alabama, and eventually the manager of the Tecumseh Iron Company near Birmingham. In 1882 the *Rome Courier* in the neighboring state of Georgia took occasion to denounce Warner as a carpet-bagger. "I have been in Alabama since 1865 and have

been a bona fide resident of the State since 1867," he
protested to a friend. "All of the $250,000 which our
company has invested in its business was brought to Alabama from other States and all of it from north of Mason and Dixon's line and yet I am a Carpet-Bagger." He
wondered: "Does not this support the charge so often
made that Northern men are not welcome in the South,
but are considered as aliens or interlopers?" But he took
heart. "The new South has its face to the Rising Sun,
and in its rapid march in material prosperity and social
progress will soon be able to leave the Courier class, with
their faces turned to the times 'before the war,' far behind."[8]

Unlike Warner, the Ohioan Albion W. Tourgée had
abandoned the effort to make a Southern career, but he
perhaps characterized Warner's experience in Alabama
as well as his own in North Carolina when, in 1884, he
wrote of the Northerner in the South:

However honestly he may endeavor to assimilate himself to his sur-
roundings, it is impossible for him to do so. In some instances the
charms of climate or exceptional success in business may for a time—
perhaps even for a lifetime—overcome the difficulties which sur-
round him. There are Northern men scattered throughout the South,
of this very type, who have been successful, and in a sense esteemed
by the communities in which they live; yet they are not a part of
them; they cannot become a part of them; and no length of resi-
dence is, as a rule, sufficient to put the Northern man or the foreign
immigrant thoroughly in harmony with Southern life.[9]

If Northerners in the South could not convert themselves into fully acceptable Southerners, it was not for
want of trying. This was as true at the beginning of the
twentieth century as it had been decades earlier, according to the Ohio-born Harvard historian Albert Bushnell
Hart, who based his opinion on more than a dozen visits
to the South. "As a rule they do not adhere to each
other," Hart said of the Northerners, "and many of them

seem to wish to hide their origin." Apparently "the Southern man and woman in the North continues to feel himself Southern to the end of his days, while the Northern man in the South tries to identify himself completely with the community in which he means to stay permanently." Hart found a reason for this phenomenon other than the inherent cogency of the Southern position. "The Southern emigrant to the North finds no door shut to him because he comes from elsewhere . . . he may criticise his [new] home and set forth the superiority of the Southland without making enemies." But "the South is not hospitable to those who plume themselves upon being Northern."

In the circumstances, the Northernizing effect of the Northern presence would seem to have been minimal. "Nevertheless," Hart surmised, "there is a strong Northern influence in the South, exercised partly through Southern men who have, either as students or as business men, become familiar with the North; partly through Northern drummers; partly through Northern business and professional men, including many Northern teachers and college professors, who are scattered throughout the South."[10]

->->X<-<-

At the turn of the century, Americans experienced a heightening sense of both nationalism and racism. These feelings rose in response to the Spanish-American War and the acquisition of overseas colonies. In the spirit of the time the Southern states were able, without serious objection from the North, to complete the disfranchising of their black citizens—a task that Southern whites had undertaken from the very beginning of Reconstruction. Far from protesting, most Northerners now showed either indifference to the Southern trend or a ready willingness to accept it and, along with it, the sentimentalities of the Lost Cause. By the early 1900s, Southernism had managed to identify itself with Americanism.

Ever since the abandonment of Reconstruction both Northern and Southern spokesmen had looked upon Negro suffrage as an obstacle to the reconciliation of the sections. E. L. Godkin, the influential editor of the New York weekly *The Nation*, also saw it as an obstacle to the Northernization of Southerners. Such a process—by which to "win them over to Northern views of politics and manners"—was the only way to "pacify the South" and effectively unite the country, Godkin wrote in 1880. "The South, in the structure of its society, in its manners and social traditions, differs nearly as much from the North as Ireland does, or Hungary, or Turkey." So while the undertaking would not be easy, neither would it be impossible. "The conversion of the Southern whites to the ways and ideas of what is called the industrial stage in social progress, which is really what has to be done to make the South peaceful, is not a more formidable task than that which the anti-slavery men had before them fifty years ago in seeking to turn Northern opinion against 'the peculiar institution.'" But Godkin was not writing with the sympathies of an abolitionist. He went on to argue that the way to "win the Southern whites" was to listen when they told why they had "such a dread of negro majorities" and to confer with them "as to the means of robbing these majorities of their terrors."[11]

Henry W. Grady made much the same point in his Boston speech of 1889. The imposition of Negro suffrage, Grady said, had given rise to the race problem and to the "seeming estrangement" of North and South. "But, sir, if the negro had not been enfranchised, the South would have been divided and the Republic united."[12] Presumably if the Negro were to be disfranchised, North and South at last would be as one.

Actually, the federal government had done nothing for more than a dozen years to enforce the Fifteenth Amendment. In the early 1890s Representative Henry Cabot Lodge of Massachusetts failed in his last attempt to pass a new enforcement act. Neither the president nor the Congress nor the Supreme Court took any step to check the Southern states when these, through state laws and constitutional amendments, deprived the blacks of the right to vote. Nor did the Republican party make an issue of it. Northern whites ought to sympathize with Southern whites, said Daniel H. Chamberlain, once a carpetbag governor of South Carolina and later a pamphleteer against black rights. By 1904, Chamberlain knew from his own experience that "with a preponderating electorate of negroes, it was never within the bounds of possibility to keep up a bearable government."[13]

No doubt Professor Hart of Harvard, who identified himself as "the son of an Ohio abolitionist," accurately described the Northern mood of 1910 when he wrote, "The North as a section is weary of the negro question . . . it is disappointed in the progress of the race both in the South and in the North . . . and less inclined than at any time during forty years to an active interference in Southern relations."[14] This forbearance on the part of Northerners, however, did not noticeably allay Southerners' suspicions and fears.

While wearying of the Negro question, the Northern public was becoming more and more enthusiastic about the romance of the Old South and the Confederacy. "Not only is the epoch of the war the favorite field of American fiction to-day, but the Confederate soldier is the popular hero," Tourgée had sadly observed in 1888. "Our literature has become not only Southern in type, but

distinctly Confederate in sympathy." Ever since the war,
in fact, Northern novelists had been adorning the theme
of reconciliation. In sixty-four war novels appearing between 1865 and 1880, the Northern heroes and hero-
ines were more than willing to let bygones be bygones,
and the Southern characters, misunderstood and mis-
understanding rather than evil in intent, displayed the
virtues of an aristocratic culture.[15]

Not till 1902, however, did the first novel come from
the pen of the South's greatest literary champion of the
Lost Cause. The book's full title was *The Leopard's Spots:
A Romance of the White Man's Burden—1865–1900*, and
the author was Thomas Dixon, Jr. In Dixon's story the
Reconstruction program figures not as a scheme to impose Northern civilization but as one to "blot out Anglo-
Saxon society and substitute African barbarism." The
North Carolina victory of the Republican-Populist coa-
lition in the 1890s is seen as a renewal of the "Africani-
sation" threat. In the election of 1900 the fictional hero
(like the real-life Charles Brantley Aycock) wins the gov-
ernorship in a campaign of Negrophobia. Then, in a
climactic speech, Dixon's hero blends the appeals of imperialism and racism while professing his undying love
for the South, "old-fashioned, mediaeval, provincial,
worshipping the dead, and raising men rather than raising money." The hero says: "The Old South fought against
the stars in their courses—the resistless tide of the rising
consciousness of Nationality and World-Mission. The
young South greets the new era and glories in its man-
hood." The White Man's Burden (as Rudyard Kipling
had recently expounded it in verse) justified both the
subjection of inferior peoples abroad and the disfran-
chisement of them at home. Now that "our flag has been
raised over ten millions of semi-barbaric black men" in
the Philippines, shall we make the same mistake we made

in Reconstruction? "Shall we repeat the farce of '67, reverse the order of nature, and make these black people
our rulers? If not, why should the African here, who is
not their equal, be allowed to imperil our life?"[16]

Dixon's villains had been Tourgée's heroes in the 1879
hit *A Fool's Errand* and in subsequent novels. Knowing
from reviews what *The Leopard's Spots* was like, Tourgée
refused to touch the book when he received a compli-
mentary copy; he carefully put it in the fireplace with a
pair of tongs. But now, in the early 1900s, Tourgée was
passé and Dixon was all the rage. A best-selling book,
The Leopard's Spots was also a success as a play, and this
together with Dixon's novel *The Clansman* (1905) formed
the basis for D. W. Griffith's widely viewed movie *The
Birth of a Nation* (1915).

Historians meanwhile were elaborating, in their less
dramatic manner, upon essentially the same theses as
were the popular novelists. The most influential scholars
of the time—James Ford Rhodes, John W. Burgess, and
William A. Dunning, all Northerners—retold the story
of Reconstruction in such a way as to make Southern
whites appear the victims of a misconceived and calami-
tous program—the imposition of Negro suffrage and,
with it, Negro rule. Northern as well as Southern writers
had only the highest praise for Robert E. Lee, who was
beginning to rival Abraham Lincoln as a national hero
in the eyes of Northerners. Clearly, in things of the imagination at least, the North was being quite thoroughly
Southernized.

While some Northerners were helping to reeducate
the North, others were failing to reeducate the South.
This reeducation had been the aim of Tourgée, as he
implied in *A Fool's Errand* and explicitly advocated in
later writings. The point of his famous book (a point
that most Southerners missed) was not the foolishness

of trying to impose upon the South the civilization of the
North, but the foolishness of trying to do so all at once.
It would be a long, slow process, Tourgée had come to
believe, and it would require *"universal enlightenment of
whites and blacks alike,"* which the federal government
would have to provide. He got nowhere, however, with
his year-in and year-out campaign to set up federally
financed and controlled schools in the South. By 1901
he was disillusioned with the idea itself. "It was a genuine fool's notion," he wrote to President Theodore Roosevelt, congratulating the president on having sat down
to eat with the black leader Booker T. Washington. "I
realize now that . . . education does not eradicate prejudice, but intensifies it."[17]

Northern philanthropists gave money for the school-
ing of Southern children, both black and white, and in
so doing they provoked fears that education could, indeed, alter feelings about race. Hence Southerners denounced as meddlers the Northerners who sponsored
such organizations as the Conference for Education in
the South. When the Conference met at Salem College
in North Carolina in 1901, Governor Aycock was on
hand to greet the delegates warmly but rather cau-
tiously. In response to a query, Aycock then sent a tele-
gram to the *New York Herald*: "If the negro is ever educated
it will be by the aid of Southern white men. The North
cannot do it. Philanthropists in the North may think
they can educate the negro without the help of Southern
whites, but they are mistaken."

During the next few years Aycock constantly appealed
to the Old South along with the New as he went about
speaking for the improvement of public education in his
state. "And with our educational advance will come a
twenty-fold industrial development," he assured a crowd
at the state fair in 1902. "Nor will the deeds of our fath-

ers be forgotten in that glorious day." He told members
of the Southern Educational Association, meeting at
Jacksonville, Florida, in 1903, that before the war
"Southern statesmen [had] directed the policies of the
nation" because the South was then an aristocracy, and
aristocrats were always well trained. Now that the South
was a democracy, its people must be equally well educated. "Universal education is therefore the imperative
and only remedy for our loss of power in the nation. But
how shall we be trained? Are we to forget the memories
of the past; to break away from our traditions; to join
with those who are clamoring for the adoption of the
convictions which we have combated for many years? I
think not."[18]

While Aycock made himself the educational leader of
his state, another North Carolinian, Walter Hines Page,
stood out as a national champion of education in the
South as a whole. Page, too, made frequent obeisance to
the past while pleading for the future. It would have
been self-defeating to do otherwise. North Carolinians
had begun to denounce Page for being "Yankeeized"
soon after his departure for the North in 1885. After
the appearance of his partly autobiographical novel *The
Southerner* in 1909—in which the protagonist remarks
that the Southerner devotes himself too much to "dis-
torted traditions" and not enough to "living ideas"—the
Chapel Hill history professor J. G. de Roulhac Hamilton
excoriated Page for his "holier than thou" attitude and
his truckling to the "sectional aspirations and aims of
New England or some other segment of the Union." In
1913 a Confederate veterans' magazine deplored Page's
appointment as ambassador to the Court of St. James.
The implication seemed to be that anyone disloyal to his
section would also be disloyal to his country.

Page, recently editor of the *Atlantic Monthly*, made one

of the most explicit presentations of his case in the May
1902 issue of that magazine. Regarding the problem of
the Southerners and their backwardness, he said: "Least
of all is it the task of imposing on these people the civilization that has been developed elsewhere (for this would
be a fool's errand indeed and in no way desirable if it
were possible)." For "no exterior or temporary influence
counts for much and the hereditary 'essence of civilization' is everything." But the Southern inheritance *is* essentially democratic and progressive. "There is no
undemocratic trait in the Southern people that is not
directly accounted for by slavery and by the results of
slavery." As for the "new impulse in public education," it
"is native, and it is nothing different from Jefferson's
creed and plan." Suppose Jefferson's educational plan
had been put into effect—"would the public schools have
prevented the growth of slavery?" Perhaps; perhaps not.
In any event, "the Southern people were deflected from
their natural development." Their natural development,
the reader is left to infer, would have paralleled that of
the Northern people.

At last, according to Page, the South was beginning to
catch up. The "great mass" of its people, the poor whites
or "white trash," had come from the same "sturdy English and Scotch-Irish stock" as the people who had originally settled much of the rest of the country. "They are
not poorer nor 'trashier' than the rural population of
New Jersey or Pennsylvania or New York or New England were several generations ago, nor than they are
now in some remote regions of these States." Having
lately revisited a Southern neighborhood he had known
twenty-five years before, Page could confidently predict
that time was "working its natural results in this American community" and twenty years hence it would be
"(except for the presence of two races) very like hundreds
of towns in the Middle West."

Page stuck by his forecast despite the opposition he
encountered in both the North and the South. A "man
of learning" in Massachusetts said to him: "The Southerners have always seemed foreigners to me. The
Northern and the Southern people are different. I do
not think they will ever work out the same ideals." And
a "man of learning" in South Carolina wrote to Page:
"The dominant elements of society in the two sections
were different from the beginning. Slavery did not make
the difference, it only emphasized it." The destruction
of slavery and of the Confederacy "did not change the
essential character of the people," and "a century hence
the South will be, in the essence of its civilization, further
from the North than it now is."[19]

Albert Bushnell Hart also differed with Page, at least
in emphasis. "The lower whites [of the South], though
advancing," Hart maintained, "are still on the average
far inferior to the similar class of white farmers of kindred
English stock in the North; and also to many of the foreigners that have come in and settled the West." Even
the "respectable Southern whites" demonstrated a
"crudeness of behavior" that one would seldom see in
the North outside the city slums. "A large proportion
. . . go armed and justify it because they expect to have
need of a weapon. Tobacco juice flows freely in hotel
corridors, in railroad stations, and even in the vestibules
of ladies' cars; profanity is rife, and fierce talk and un-
bridled denunciations, principally of black people." These
impressions of a Northern traveler in the South, published in 1910, were reminiscent of those of other travelers sixty or seventy years before. In all the intervening
time, the South and Southerners had apparently changed
but little in some respects.

Certainly, as the First World War approached, Northerners and Southerners typically had rather different
conceptions of patriotism. Hart used an anecdote to il-

lustrate the difference. At a recent Phi Beta Kappa din-
ner in Cambridge the president of the University of North
Carolina, George T. Winston, had said: "I love North
Carolina, I ought to love that State, because it is my
native country!" Harvard President Charles W. Eliot replied: "President Winston says that North Carolina is his
native country; gentlemen, it's *our* native country." It
seemed to Hart that the North had long "been disposed
to consider itself the characteristic United States," and
the South to look upon itself as "a unit within a larger
unit" and as somehow "set apart."[20] Yet it still seemed to
many Southerners that the South was more truly American than the rest of the nation, since the South, having
changed less, remained more nearly like the original republic.

In 1918, as in 1898, war brought Northerners and
Southerners together against a foreign foe. Once again,
neither the heightened nationalism nor the shared experience was enough to overcome the Southern sense of
differentness and separateness. Nor did the postwar ac-
celeration of industrial growth in the South achieve that
end. During the 1920s and 1930s the region underwent
a revival of nostalgia and an intensification of self-
consciousness, as evidenced by the founding of such societies as the Southern Economics Association in 1929
and the Southern Historical Association in 1934. Southernism and superpatriotism reinforced one another. Together, they fostered the growth of the Ku Klux Klan
after the fictions of Thomas Dixon had inspired its re-
founding in Atlanta in 1915. The spread of the Klan
throughout the country was one of many indications that,

spiritually, there continued to be less Northernization of the South than Southernization of the North.

The few deliberate Northernizers of the 1920s were not organized groups or government agencies but self-appointed individuals—and rather quixotic ones at that. Foremost among the tilters at Southern windmills rode H. L. Mencken, editor of the iconoclastic magazines *Smart Set* and *American Mercury*. Mencken first struck in 1917 with his article "The Sahara of the Bozart," in which he described the South as a land without literature or learning, a wilderness of "Baptist and Methodist barbarism," a hopeless "Bible Belt." By 1924 he was beginning to feel considerable hope. "Fundamentalism, Ku Kluxry, revivals, lynchings, hog wallow politics—these are the things that always occur to a northerner when he thinks of the south," Mencken then wrote, but he hastened to add: "All over the south the minority is emancipating itself and having its say, and in more than one state it is making cruel practice upon the poor whites and their pastors. What one observes is the rise of a new aristocracy, and it is sounder than the old one because it is based upon better brains."[21]

At that time the most explicit (and most fantastic) Northern proposal for dealing with the South came from Frank Tannenbaum, then a brash young social scientist from New York City. In *The Darker Phases of the South* (1924) Tannenbaum said a fanatical devotion to "Anglo-Saxon ideals, racial integrity, and religious purity" distinguished and darkened the region. "I have seen it go to the extent of regretting the entering of young Southerners in Northern Universities on the ground that their religious faith is undermined." To break down this exclusive spirit, Tannenbaum proposed that the federal government promote the migration of Southern blacks to the North and encourage the settlement of European

immigrants in the South. The "incoming of large masses
of foreigners with their varied racial strains, their different cultures, their many tongues, their different religious faiths," he argued, would eventually destroy the
Southern whites' "morbid pride of race" and "bitter sense
of religious righteousness."[22] No doubt social engineer-
ing of that kind would have been a promising means of
making the South more nearly like the North—had there
been even the remotest possibility that Calvin Coolidge's
administration would have undertaken such a program.

No such plan but only a plea for eliminating the "pro-
vincialism and sectional prejudices of the ruling class in
the South" came from William H. Skaggs, an Alabamian
by birth and upbringing and a New Yorker by choice. In
The Southern Oligarchy (1924) Skaggs expressed his concern that the United States had "almost ceased to be a
nation" because, on the one hand, a "large percentage
of the alien element" was not being assimilated and because, on the other hand, the Southern oligarchs were
unable or unwilling to "rise above their sectional prejudices and race hatred." This "prevalence of sectionalism" in the South was certainly not "due to attacks from
without," he contended. "No party, faction, or political
leader, outside the Southern States, at least since the
Spanish-American war, has attempted to arouse sectional animosities." One evidence of the prevailing kind
of sectionalism, according to Skaggs, was the fact that,
in the Sixty-fifth Congress, there were no members from
Southern states who had been born in the North, but
"there were ten Senators from Northern States who were
born in the South."[23]

How little effect such writers as Mencken, Tannenbaum, and Skaggs were having—how little the South
was changing in the ways they advocated—one can gather
from a book that appeared in 1927 under the title *The*

Changing South. The author, William J. Robertson, a native Virginian and a Roanoke newspaperman, conceded that a "noteworthy influence" in parts of the region was the Northerner who had settled there. "Unlike his 'carpetbagger' predecessor, he usually is a wealthy man who finds in the South the climate, scenery and environment which appeals to him as a home site." In saying that, Robertson betrayed an inexact knowledge of the historical carpetbagger, but he seemed in tune with history when he observed: "The Northerners who migrate to the South . . . retain much of their loyalty to the North, but as years pass they assimilate the Southern traditions and ideals, and their children are as loyal to the South, in time, as are the children of the natives." Despite the continuing arrival of Northerners, despite the accelerating economic change, the South was still dedicated to "three fundamental attitudes" which "for more than three score years" had "made her a nation within a nation." These attitudes were an insistence on one-party politics, a devotion to the Lost Cause, and a refusal to "recognize the rights of the Negro race."[24] A year after Robertson's book appeared, the insistence on one-party politics seemed to give way when Herbert Hoover cracked the Solid South, but in fact the principle was only in abeyance.

Ineffective though the shafts from the North were, some Southerners perceived a danger, more insidious than it had been for many years, impending from that direction. Most nervous and most articulate were the self-styled Agrarians—scholars and aesthetes with a Vanderbilt connection, a dozen of whom contributed to the manifesto *I'll Take My Stand* (1930). The authors played variations on the theme of industrialism versus agrarianism, evil versus good, North versus South.

One of the twelve, the historian F. L. Owsley, main-

tained that the Civil War had been a "struggle between
an agrarian and an industrial civilization," and he indicated that the war was still going on. After the surrender
at Appomattox, according to Owsley, the conquerors
turned the former Confederate states "over to the three
millions of former slaves, some of whom could still remember the taste of human flesh and the bulk of them
hardly three generations removed from cannibalism,"
for them to pillage throughout ten years under the
incitement of "savage political leaders like Thaddeus
Stevens" and under the guidance of contemptible
carpetbaggers and scalawags. Even that was not enough
to satisfy the "crusading, standardizing" urge of the vic-
tors. "After the South had been conquered by war and
humiliated and impoverished by peace, there appeared
still to remain something which made the South different—something intangible, incomprehensible, in the
realm of the spirit. That too must be invaded and destroyed; so there commenced a second war of conquest,
the conquest of the Southern mind, calculated to remake every Southern opinion, to impose the Northern
way of life and thought upon the South."

Among the other contributors to *I'll Take My Stand*,
the poet John Gould Fletcher deplored the public school
system on the grounds that it was eroding the "traditions
of leisure, of culture, of intellectual tolerance and sane
kindliness" that had survived from the Old South.
Fletcher warned: "if the present system persists, in another generation nothing will remain of the local color,
the diversity, the humanity, the charm of our South, and
we will become assimilated outwardly and inwardly to
the street gangs of New York and Chicago." The novelist
Stark Young took what comfort he could from noting
that the South, whose manners and customs had always
come "from the top downward," never "sought the me-

chanical perfection in domestic living—the vulgarities in plumbing competition, for example"—that interested "so much of America now" but had no place in "any aristocratic life in Europe."[25]

In the 1920s and 1930s, as in earlier decades, the South (or at least her intellectuals) remained divided on the question of progress. The backward-looking Agrarians now faced the opposition of the forward-looking Regionalists. Howard W. Odum, the leader of the Regionalists, had no use for the "nostalgic yearnings" and the "little realism" of the Agrarians, though he shared some of their misconceptions about the past. As a Chapel Hill professor, the Georgia-born Odum had founded the *Journal of Social Forces* and the Institute for Research in Social Sciences to encourage studies that might have the practical effect of raising the level of Southern life and thought. Odum's work caught the attention of H. L. Mencken and led to his 1924 expression of optimism about the Southern future. "He remains a thorough southerner, wholly devoted to the south," Mencken wrote in praise of Odum. "What he has introduced down there is simply the doctrine that the ancient evasions . . . the hoary sentimentalities have outlived their protective usefulness."[26]

Odum summed up his findings in the fact-filled tome *Southern Regions of the United States* (1936). The plural *Regions* in the title was significant. "There is no longer in the United States any single entity which may be designated 'the South,'" Odum believed. There were a Southeast and a Southwest, and within the Southeast there were important variations from state to state. "'Many states, many souths' . . . Florida and Arkansas are likely to be more different, the one from the other, than Virginia from Maryland or Pennsylvania; Mississippi more different from North Carolina than Carolina is from

Ohio." Odum's tables of statistics showed the Southern regions lagging behind the others (Northeast, Northwest, Middle States, Far West) in most measures of the quality of life. One notable fact: as of 1930, the number of people born elsewhere and living in the Southeast was only 400,000; the number born in the Southeast and living elsewhere was 3,800,000—more than nine times as many! Despite the facts, Southerners gained self-consciousness and self-satisfaction, Odum intimated, from the "demagogic thunder" of preachers and politicians, whose reiterated message was "Republicans and yankees and northern city folks are meddlers and corrupters of the South."[27]

Already the Great Depression and the New Deal were exacerbating Southern sensitivity. Relief and make-work programs such as the WPA had the odor of abolitionism about them, since they tended to emancipate blacks from low-paid domestic service by offering alternative sources of income. The NRA, with its production limits and wage minimums, also seemed to have anti-Southern implications. "You know," the Chattanooga newspaperman George Fort Milton wrote to Franklin D. Roosevelt's secretary of commerce in 1934, "that a great many of our Southern industrialists suspect . . . that much of the glee about NRA is because it is going to permit obsolete units of the north and east to better themselves at the expense of the South." A Tennessee businessman informed the Southern Pine Association: "As a matter of fact the N.R.A. was devised, to a very large extent, to reform the South. . . . General [Hugh S.] Johnson [NRA administrator] practically told me that when he said, 'We don't propose to allow the Negro labor of the South to debase the living standards of the rest of the country.'"[28]

The crowning proof of a Northern plot presumably inhered in the *Report on the Economic Conditions of the*

South, which the federal government published in 1938. The effect was ironic. An anti-Southern gesture had been the farthest thing from President Roosevelt's mind when he commissioned the report and declared: "It is my conviction that the South presents right now the Nation's No. 1 economic problem—the Nation's problem, not merely the South's." Materials for the study came from Odum and other Southern experts. And the report itself emphasized the charge that the South was the victim of Northern exploitation, that the region's poverty was due to high tariffs, discriminatory freight rates, and the profiteering of "outside financiers."

But some of the evidences of poverty were shocking to Southern sensibilities—except perhaps to those of persons like Stark Young, with his aristocratic contempt for the "vulgarities" of modern plumbing. "In extensive rural districts there are not only no indoor flush toilets," the study revealed, "but no outdoor privies even of the most primitive sort."[29] The very designation of "No. 1 economic problem" rankled in many minds. The majority of Southern newspapers denounced the report, as the Charlotte journalist Wilbur J. Cash noted soon afterward. "And the Southern States Industrial Council, an organization made up of many of the most important business men of the South, including some of those who are supposed to be most liberal, assailed it as a pack of falsehoods invented out of Yankee and New Deal malice, with a view to discrediting and crippling Progress in the South." So wrote Cash, disapprovingly, of those Southerners who in 1938 bristled at the specter of Northern malevolence.

Yet Cash himself, in his classic *The Mind of the South* (1940), took much the same view of the history of North-South relations as a whole. All along, he contended, there had been "that will to win the South from its divergence

and bring it into the flow of the nation," that will which
"was the most fundamental drive behind the Yankee's
behavior." Eloquently, if extravagantly, Cash said with
reference to Reconstruction: "Not Ireland nor Poland,
not Finland nor Bohemia, not one of the countries which
prove the truth that there is no more sure way to make
a nation than the brutal oppression of an honorably de-
feated and disarmed people—not one of these, for all
the massacres, the pillage, and the rapes to which they
have so often been subjected, was ever so pointedly taken
in the very core of its being as was the South." Conse-
quently, Southerners intensified their "old terrified
truculence toward new ideas from the outside," saw the
"entire body of the South's troubles" as "flowing out of
Yankee civilization and the Yankee mind," and viewed
"every idea originated by the Yankee or bearing the stamp
of his acceptance as containing within itself the old im-
placable will to coerce and destroy." Out of this fear arose,
in one way or another, such familiar Southern traits as
religious conservatism, high-flown political oratory, the
tendency to violence and mob action, even the "Southern rape complex." In other words, according to Cash,
the long effort to Northernize had made the South what
it was.[30]

Here was a sophisticated reaffirmation of the Dunning and Owsley slant on Southern history. And here
was a compelling reassertion of Southern identity at a
time when, with Pearl Harbor in the offing, world events
seemed to call for the utmost in national unity. Paradox-
ically, the South, the most sectionalist part of the country, also appeared in these prewar years to be the most
nationalistic, the most "interventionist," the most eager
to defend democracy abroad—though not to expand it
at home.

During and after the Second World War the South began, in demographic and economic development, to ap-
proximate the North more closely than ever. Whether it
did the same in spirit and essence—or ought to do so—
remained a matter of debate.

The Second World War, like the First, greatly stimu-
lated the northward movement of Southern blacks. For
decades they had accounted for most of the South's population loss, and by 1960 they were as numerous outside
the region as in it. By this time, the migration of whites
to the South was beginning to offset the exodus of blacks
from it. In 1960 more than 3 million Northern-born
whites were living in the South, while fewer than 3.8
million Southern-born whites were living in the North.
During the next two decades the South was to make
increasing population gains from the arrival of Northerners.

Meanwhile the people staying in the South were
crowding more and more into cities. By 1960 the population was 58 percent urban, and by 1970 nearly 65
percent urban. Fewer than 8 percent (in the former
Confederate states) continued to live on farms. Those
Southern farmers—like many of their Northern coun-
terparts—produced little or no cotton and large quan-
tities of poultry, eggs, cattle, and dairy products. During
the wartime and early postwar years metropolitan areas
grew much faster in the South than in the country as a
whole, and so did the economy. Building construction,
urban and suburban, was rapidly altering the face if not
the soul of the South.[31]

To some Southern intellectuals of the period, these
trends were no more reassuring than those of the 1920s

had been to the Agrarians. "All indications are that the bulldozer will leave a deeper mark upon the land than did the carpetbagger," the Arkansas-born historian C. Vann Woodward noted with regret in 1958. "The threat of becoming 'indistinguishable,' of being submerged under a national steamroller, has haunted the mind of the South for a long time." Obviously it still haunted the mind of Woodward. He took what reassurance he could from the one thing about the South that was "immune from the disintegrating effect"—the South's history or, rather, its "collective experience" of poverty, defeat, and guilt, which must remain forever distinct from the Northern or American tradition of wealth, success, and innocence. Fourteen years later Woodward seemed to have grown even more apprehensive. "We are, in fact, still living with the progressive realization of Grady's dream of a Yankeefied South," he said at a Florida symposium in 1972. "Every new throughway, every new supermarket, every central city is an extension of it. The full horror of it is suggested only slightly by a drive between Tampa and Clearwater. I wonder if what the South really wants is uncritical emulation of the North."[32]

Defenders of Southernism had to contend not only with this new onslaught of Yankee commercialism but also, after the Supreme Court's 1954 decision in *Brown* v. *Board of Education*, with "fresh assaults" upon the South's "regime and its order of values" in respect to race. "All the while it [the South] has known that what grudging respect it has obtained from the North has come because the South has maintained the standards of white civilization," wrote Richard M. Weaver, a North Carolina native teaching English at the University of Chicago, in 1957. "It knows that if it were to accept without reservation the dictates of the Supreme Court, it might be turned into something like those 'mixed sections' found in large Northern cities." According to Weaver, the North had always been Faustian, eager to "make over things in its own image," and the South had always been Apollonian, or Classical. "Under the banner first of reform and then of progress, the North challenged the right to continue of a civilization based on the Classical ideal of fixity and stability." In her determination to "preserve her character and autonomy," the South "might be viewed as an American Ireland, Poland, or Armenia."

Agreeing with Weaver, another English professor, the Nashville-born Walter Sullivan of Vanderbilt, commented further that the desegregation issue was alienating the sections. "Since the ante-bellum days, seldom has the South been nearer the rest of the nation in spirit than it was in the years immediately following World War II," Sullivan observed. "Now, in the mid-fifties, the situation is different." A majority of white Southerners are bound to "oppose any change at all that they themselves have not initiated; they resent Northern interference as hypocritical and officious and in many cases downright dishonest, in view of contemporary race relations in the North." Sullivan consoled himself with the thought that, for more than a hundred years, resistance to Northern interference had kept the South uniquely Southern, and such resistance could be expected to continue to do so. This, Sullivan confessed, might be "a result of sectional paranoia," but it was far better than submergence in "the material ethics of a city oriented civilization."[33]

Paranoia was indeed the key to Southern character, according to a sympathetic analysis by the Alabama-born historian Sheldon Hackney. "Though southerners have many other identities," Hackney concluded in 1969, "they are likely to be most conscious of being southerners when they are defending their region against attack from out-

side forces: abolitionists, the Union Army, carpetbaggers, Wall Street and Pittsburgh, civil rights agitators,
the federal government, feminism, socialism, trade-
unionism, Darwinism, Communism, atheism, daylight-
saving time, and other by-products of modernity." To be
Southern, then, was to have "a feeling of persecution," a
feeling based on history or, at any rate, on the Southerners' perception of the past.[34]

Again, however, as so often before, Southerners reacted
in more than one way, and not all of them now insisted
on taking a stand against civil rights agitators, or on defining Southernism in racist terms, or even on discover-
ing fundamental differences between North and South.
"Will history repeat itself?" asked the Southern-born
Berkeley historian Charles G. Sellers in 1960. "Will the
Sumter centennial find Southerners once again defining
their Southernism in desperate, unreasoning revolt
against the larger society of which they have always been
a part, against social values which they have always
shared?" Another native Southerner teaching in the
North, Thomas P. Govan, argued that cultural distinctions between North and South had never been more
than minor, that the only important cause of sectional
difference and conflict had been slavery, and that the
South's "return to the nation was not an abandonment
of its ancient tradition, but a return to it."[35]

A number of (white) Southern advocates of civil rights
agreed with Howard Zinn, a New York City native who
had taught at Spelman College, that the "Southern mystique" was disappearing, that the South in its racism and
other unpleasant characteristics was not different but
was "really the *essence* of the nation," and that the assumption of basic difference merely fed "self-
righteousness in the North." The Mississippian Frank E.
Smith (who titled his 1965 book *Look Away from Dixie*, in

obvious reply to the 1930 *I'll Take My Stand*) thought the real difference insignificant. "The South as a symbol has absorbed so much of the energy and ability of white Southerners through the past century," he believed, "that it is worth considering whether the very concept of the term has any future value for the nation, or even for those who live in the South." Pat Watters, director of the biracial Southern Regional Council, said in 1969 that he "started out to write about the South as it has usually been done, treating the region as a separate entity," but soon realized that recent changes had ended "forever whatever there remained (or ever had been) of self-containment, of separateness in the South from the rest of the nation."[36]

Writing on the "Americanization of Dixie" (1971), the Atlanta journalist Joseph B. Cumming, Jr., picked up the theme that the rest of the nation had been "seeing its own flaws in the South" and had been "laying in moral commitments" for itself. "But now the South has adopted what it likes to call the subtle ways of segregation of the North," Cumming reported. And "now that the South is over, its racism Americanized," he asked, "will we finally shed this militant sectionalism?" The Tennessean John Egerton elaborated (1973) on the thesis that "the Americanization of Dixie and the Southernization of America are homogenizing processes" in which the South and the rest of the country "are sharing and spreading the worst in each other." By the 1970s the Louisiana novelist Walker Percy had come to regard himself as an American writer rather than a Southern one, and apparently he was not greatly troubled to remark: "I sometimes think that some parts of the South are more like the North than the North itself."[37]

While many white liberals of the South no longer saw much, if any, regional distinctiveness, others continued

to find noteworthy evidence of it. To strengthen their
case, these others made use of the suddenly fashionable
concepts of ethnicity and cultural pluralism. Afro-
Americans, as an ethnic group, were asserting a separate
identity and a cultural autonomy; so were aboriginal,
Hispanic, and Oriental Americans. Even the descendants of European immigrants—Irish, Italian, Slovak,
Polish, Hungarian, and so on—were beginning to identify themselves as "ethnics." Why should not white
Southerners (and not merely those of Appalachia) do
the same? After all, commentators for many generations
had compared them to the oppressed nationals of such
places as Ireland, Poland, and Armenia.

White Southerners was the title of a volume that appeared in 1970 in a sociological series on "Ethnic Groups
in Comparative Perspective." The author, Lewis M. Killian, a Georgia-born sociologist at the University of Massachusetts, pointed out that both Northerners in the South
and Southerners in the North remained consciously and
identifiably alien: "The white Southerner of Yankee origin is, like the Jew, conscious of his marginality." In the
North the poor whites from the South—the "hillbillies"—were, according to a Detroit public opinion sur-
vey, identified as "undesirable people" even more
frequently than were transients or drifters, Negroes, or
foreigners. The "relatively affluent migrants" from the
South, suffering less discrimination, did not form a co-
hesive group as did the hillbillies, but neither did they
forget that they were Southerners. "As long as they retain their southern accents, they are likely to be reminded of their origin in ways that are often amusing
but sometimes infuriating." Apparently Killian here was
testifying from his own experience, and he went on to
explain from his sociological expertise: "Pluralism rep-
resents the effort of a group to cope with the problem

of preserving its distinctive, historical identity when the demands of national unity threaten to override subsocietal loyalties." In coping with this problem, white Southerners, as a "self-conscious minority," were "the nation's oldest pluralists."[38]

In *The Enduring South: Subcultural Persistence in Mass Society* (1972) another Southern sociologist, John Shelton Reed of Chapel Hill, agreed essentially with Killian. "Southerners' differences from the American mainstream have been similar in kind, if not degree, to those of the immigrant ethnic groups," Reed declared. He contributed to the argument additional evidence he had gathered from an analysis of responses to nationwide public opinion polls. In these responses he found what he thought were significant "North-South differences of three sorts: differences in attachment to the local community, in attitudes toward the private use of force and violence, and in religious and quasi-religious beliefs and practices." Reed saw no reason to believe that industrialization or "modernization" would soon, if ever, eliminate regional differences and bring about national uniformity, since extreme cultural dissimilarities could and did persist within the modern industrial world. "For a long time to come," he predicted, "we can expect that the South will be something more than simply the lower right-hand part of the country."[39]

George B. Tindall, a migrant from South to North Carolina, chose "The Ethnic Southerners" as the topic of his presidential address to the Southern Historical Association in 1973—and he was not talking about immigrant groups in the South. On ethnic and other grounds Tindall, too, was confident that the South was not about to disappear. Its performance was still, as always, "less a disappearing act than a transformation scene." For two centuries it had been repeatedly changing its shape, like Proteus. Now it was undergoing yet another transformation as the "Sun Belt" emerged on the Southern horizon of the United States, "reaching from coast to coast, its economy battening on 'agribusiness,' defense, technology, oil, real estate, tourism, and leisure." Tindall made bold to prophesy: "Reincarnated · as the imperial Sun Belt, the region is about to assume a new role—as arbiter of the national destiny."[40]

North and South were reversing positions in more ways than one, according to the University of Virginia historian Paul M. Gaston. "The South, in fact, has been asked to play a remarkable new role as model for the nation to emulate," he announced in 1973. Gone now were the "old and comforting myths of American invincibility, opportunity, and virtue." Their destruction had come about in consequence of race riots and resistance to school desegregation in Northern cities, the horrors and frustrations of the Vietnam war, and then the revelation of the Watergate scandals. The heroes of Watergate turned out to be what Northerners had always considered a low breed, that is, Southern politicians— Senators Ervin, Baker, and Talmadge. Losing confidence in the ancient verities, and increasingly concerned about crime, pollution, anomie, and other ills, "Americans began to look differently at the South," for they now realized that Southerners "might be able, really, to show how men may live harmoniously in a complex, interracial, urban society." Southernization of the North and not Northernization of the South, Gaston thus implied, ought to be the ideal.[41]

Looking ahead to the 1980s, some in both North and South questioned, from opposing points of view, the economic benefits of Northernization. In a 1981 paper entitled "The Second War between the States," Wisconsin Congressman Les Aspin argued that the federal government, through tax writeoffs and defense expenditures, was already doing too much to enrich the "Sun Belt" states at the expense of the "Frost Belt" states. A 1981 report on the future of the South warned: "By becoming more like the nation, the South inevitably is losing some of the advantages it has had over other parts of the country in attracting population, business and industry." The authors of this report were fairly confident that the region would retain its distinctiveness, though they seemed unsure as to just what its distinctiveness consisted of. They were content to say: "The lists of Southern idiosyncrasies are endless, the sum of them impossible to describe."[42]

And so, after two hundred years, the idea of Northernizing the South, as a project to be either welcomed or resisted, continued to live on. Whether the South itself still lived on—the South as a basically and truly distinct entity—was another question.

Notes

ONE
Two Civilizations—or One?
1780s–1850s

1. Jefferson to the Marquis de Chastellux, September 2, 1785, in *The Papers of Thomas Jefferson*, ed. Julian P. Boyd, vol. 8 (Princeton: Princeton University Press, 1953), pp. 467–68.

2. *Journal of the Federal Convention Kept by James Madison*, ed. E. H. Scott (1840; reprint ed., Chicago: Albert, Scott, 1893), pp. 578–83, 626–30.

3. *Journal of William Maclay, United States Senator from Pennsylvania, 1789–1791*, ed. Edgar S. Maclay (New York: D. Appleton, 1890), pp. 5, 20, 196–97, 210, 217, 223, 315, 341–42.

4. *Annals of Congress: The Debates and Proceedings of the Congress of the United States*, 16th Cong., 1st sess., December 6, 1819–May 15, 1820 (Washington: Gales and Seaton, 1855), cols. 135–36, 159–62, 268–70.

5. *Memoirs of John Quincy Adams, Comprising Portions of His Diary from 1795 to 1848*, ed. Charles Francis Adams, 12 vols. (Philadelphia: J. B. Lippincott, 1874–77), 5: 10–12.

6. Glover Moore, *The Missouri Controversy, 1819–1821* (1953; reprint ed., Lexington: University of Kentucky Press, 1966), pp. 254–57.

7. Francis and Theresa Pulszky, *White Red Black: Sketches of Society in the United States during the Visit of Their Guest* [Louis Kossuth] 3 vols. (1853; reprint ed., New York: Negro Universities Press, 1968), 3: 25.

8. Thomas Hamilton, *Men and Manners in America* (1833; reprint ed., New York: Russell & Russell, 1968), pp. 125–26, 350–51. On English views of the superiority of Southerners with respect to manners, wit, and vivacity, see Jane Louise Mesick, *The English Traveller in America, 1785–1835* (1922; reprint ed., Westport, Conn.: Green-

wood Press, 1970), pp. 67–70 and passim; and Max Berger, *The British Traveller in America, 1836–1860* (New York: Columbia University Press, 1943), p. 118 and passim.

9. D. J. McCord, "South—How Affected by Her Slave Institutions—Slavery at the South—What Elements of Character and Civilization It Develops, and How They Compare with Those of the North," in J[ames]. D. B. De Bow, ed., *The Industrial Resources, Statistics, Etc., of the United States, and More Particularly of the Southern and Western States*, 3 vols. (1852; reprint ed., New York: Augustus M. Kelley, 1966), 3: 62–70; George Fitzhugh, *Sociology for the South, or the Failure of Free Society* (1854; reprint ed., New York: Burt Franklin, 1965), p. 244.

10. Frederick Law Olmsted, *The Cotton Kingdom: A Traveller's Observations on Cotton and Slavery in the American Slave States, Based upon Three Former Volumes of Journeys and Investigations by the Same Author* (1861; reprint ed., New York: Alfred A. Knopf, 1953), pp. 548–50.

11. Daniel R. Hundley, *Social Relations in Our Southern States* (1860; reprint ed., Baton Rouge: Louisiana State University Press, 1979), pp. 129–30. Hundley preferred to think of the Yankee as a type originating anywhere in the country, not exclusively in a certain part of it. He conceded that there were probably more Yankees in New England than anywhere else, but he emphasized that not all New Englanders were (by his definition) Yankees. He was especially interested in the "Southern Yankee," and by this he meant not a newcomer from the North, but a native of the South. The Southern Yankee, he said, was the "meanest" and most detestable of the lot, yet was "not altogether without redeeming qualities." As the Northern Yankee had been "the main instrument in advancing the North to her present proud position, as a great manufacturing, inventive, and commercial community," so the Southern Yankee had "contributed no little to the present unprecedented prosperity of the Slave States" (*Social Relations*, pp. 130–39, 155–57). Regardless of Hundley's views, most of his fellow Southerners were sure that, on the whole, Northerners closely fit the Yankee stereotype and Southerners were quite different.

12. James Stirling, *Letters from the Slave States* (London: John W. Parker and Son, 1857), pp. 101–2.

13. James S. Buckingham, *America: Historical, Statistic, and Descriptive*, 3 vols. (London: Fisher, Son & Co., 1841), 2: 271.

14. Stirling, *Slave States*, pp. 272–73; Olmsted, *Cotton Kingdom*, p. 555; Henry B. Whipple, *Bishop Whipple's Southern Diary, 1843–1844*,

ed. L. B. Shippee (Minneapolis: University of Minnesota Press, 1937), pp. 30–31, 40; John S. C. Abbott, *South and North; or, Impressions Received during a Trip to Cuba and the South* (New York: Abbot & Abbot, 1860), pp. 85–87, 114.

15. Abbott, *South and North*, p. 75; Alexis de Tocqueville, *Democracy in America*, trans. Henry Reeve, 2 vols. (1835–40; reprint ed., New York: D. Appleton, 1904), 1: 383; Sir E. R. Sullivan, *Rambles and Scrambles in North and South America* (London, 1853), quoted in Berger, *British Traveller*, pp. 124–25; Pulszka, *Red White Black*, 3: 25.

16. Howard R. Floan, *The South in Northern Eyes, 1831–1861* (Austin: University of Texas Press, 1958), pp. 51–58.

17. Whipple, *Southern Diary*, pp. 31, 41–42, 60; Tocqueville, *Democracy in America*, 1: 386–89; Stirling, *Slave States*, pp. 64–65, 177–78; Earl of Carlisle (G. W. F. Howard), *Travels in America* (New York, 1851), quoted in Berger, *British Traveller*, pp. 43–44; Olmsted, *Cotton Kingdom*, pp. 553–55.

18. Tocqueville, *Democracy in America*, 1: 386; Floan, *South in Northern Eyes*, pp. 12–13; Stirling, *Slave States*, pp. 60–63, 235, 353; *Burlington Daily Times* (Vt.), May 14, 1861, quoted in Howard C. Perkins, ed., *Northern Editorials on Secession*, 2 vols. (New York: D. Appleton-Century, 1942), 1: 531–33; Abbott, *South and North*, pp. 120–21, 127–28, 160–61; Whipple, *Southern Diary*, p. 40. See also (Baron) Frederick von Raumer, *America and the American People*, trans. William W. Turner (New York: J. and H. G. Langley, 1846), p. 119.

19. Abbott, *South and North*, pp. 104–11, 330–31; James D. B. De Bow, "The Non-Slaveholders of the South: Their Interest in the Present Sectional Controversy Identical with That of the Slaveholders," *De Bow's Review* 30 (January 1861): 73.

20. Tocqueville, *Democracy in America*, 1: 444.

21. [George Lewis Prentiss, ed.,] *A Memoir of S. S. Prentiss*, 2 vols. (1855; reprint ed., New York: Charles Scribner's Sons, 1879), 1: 70–71; 2: 407–8, 541–42. See also Dallas C. Dickey, *Seargent S. Prentiss: Whig Orator of the Old South* (Baton Rouge: Louisiana State University Press, 1945).

22. Hundley, *Social Relations*, p. 136; Moore, *Missouri Controversy*, p. 257; John K. Bettersworth, *Confederate Mississippi: The People and Policies of a Cotton State in Wartime* (Baton Rouge: Louisiana State University Press, 1943), p. 1; Fletcher M. Green, *The Role of the Yankee in the Old South* (Athens: University of Georgia Press, 1972), pp. 4–6, 39, 68, 122–23, 131–32.

23. The exact figures were 609,223 and 205,924, as given in Hin-

ton Rowan Helper, *The Impending Crisis of the South: How to Meet It* (1857; reprint ed., New York: A. B. Burdick, 1860), p. 304.

24. Eric Foner, *Free Soil, Free Labor, Free Men: The Ideology of the Republican Party before the Civil War* (New York: Oxford University Press, 1970), pp. 48–51, 54, 56; Stirling, *Slave States*, pp. 76–77; [Wendell P. Garrison,] *William Lloyd Garrison, 1805–1879: The Story of His Life Told by His Children*, 4 vols. (New York: Century, 1889), 3: 48.

25. Stirling, *Slave States*, pp. 76–77; Floan, *South in Northern Eyes*, pp. 12–13; Foner, *Free Soil*, pp. 51–54, 69–71.

26. Olmsted, *Cotton Kingdom*, pp. 508–9; Abbott, *South and North*, pp. 120–21, 160–61, 225.

27. See Wilbur J. Cash, *The Mind of the South* (1941; reprint ed., Garden City, N.Y.: Doubleday, 1954), pp. 74–75; William R. Taylor, *Cavalier and Yankee: The Old South and American National Character* (1961; reprint ed., Garden City, N.Y.: Doubleday, 1963), pp. 287–89, 313–14. Foner points out that Taylor exaggerates the extent to which Northerners had "a preference for the genteel aristocrat over the predatory businessman" (*Free Soil*, p. 68).

28. Whipple, *Southern Diary*, pp. 80–81; Cash, *Mind of the South*, pp. 91–92, quoting Thornwell.

29. Quoted in Charles G. Sellers, ed., *The Southerner as American* (Chapel Hill: University of North Carolina Press, 1960), p. viii.

30. De Bow, *Industrial Resources*, 3: 93–95.

31. See, for example, the resolution of the South Central Agricultural Society of Georgia, as quoted in Pulszka, *White Red Black*, 3: 17; and a set of resolutions from an undated and unidentified Alabama newspaper, as quoted in De Bow, *Industrial Resources*, 3: 122–23.

32. De Bow, "The South and the Union—Resources and Wealth of the South, and What She Has Contributed towards the Growth of the Nation," in De Bow, *Industrial Resources*, 3: 70–76.

33. Fitzhugh, *Sociology for the South*, pp. 45, 94, 244, 256–57, 306.

34. John Hope Franklin, *A Southern Odyssey: Travelers in the Antebellum North* (Baton Rouge: Louisiana State University Press, 1976), pp. 211–20; John McCardell, *The Idea of a Southern Nation: Southern Nationalists and Southern Nationalism, 1830–1860* (New York: W. W. Norton, 1979), p. 166; Taylor, *Cavalier and Yankee*, pp. 258–59.

35. Helper, *Impending Crisis*, pp. 11–12, 21–22, 42–43, 56–57, 60, 364–65.

36. J. Quitman Moore, "National Characteristics—the Issues of

the Day," *De Bow's Review* 30 (January 1861): 42, 46, and an anonymous Virginian on Southern feelings of inferiority, ibid. (May-June 1861): 606–10.

37. *Democratic Standard*, November 24, 1860; *Cincinnati Daily Press*, February 1, 1861; *Burlington Daily Times*, May 14, 1861, all quoted in Perkins, *Northern Editorials on Secession*, 1: 100–101, 531–33; 2: 585.

TWO

Reconstruction without Regeneration

1860s–1870s

1. *New York Times*, May 10, 1861, quoted in Perkins, *Northern Editorials on Secession* 2: 831–33. See also the Concord *New Hampshire Patriot and State Gazette*, May 8, 1861, ibid., 2: 830–31.

2. *The Liberator*, 31: 74, quoted in [Garrison,] *William Lloyd Garrison*, 4:22–23; Orestes A. Brownson, *Brownson on the Rebellion* (St. Louis, 1861), in Frank Freidel, ed., *Union Pamphlets of the Civil War, 1861–1865*, 2 vols. (Cambridge: Harvard University Press, 1967), 1: 159–60.

3. *The Works of Oliver Wendell Holmes*, 13 vols. (Boston: Houghton Mifflin, 1892), 8: 85–86.

4. Francis Parkman to the editors, *Boston Daily Advertiser*, July 14, 1863, quoted in Richard D. Rust, ed., *Glory and Pathos: Responses of Nineteenth-Century American Authors to the Civil War* (Boston: Holbrook Press, 1970), pp. 79–82.

5. Clement L. Vallandigham, "The Great Civil War in America," speech in the House of Representatives, January 14, 1863, reprinted in Freidel, *Union Pamphlets*, 2: 722–25.

6. George F. Comstock, "Let Us Reason Together" (New York, 1864) and Robert C. Winthrop, "The Election of McClellan the Only Hope for Union and Peace" (speech at New London, Conn., October 18, 1864), in Freidel, *Union Pamphlets*, 2: 900, 1101.

7. Wendell Phillips, "The War for the Union: A Lecture" (New York, 1862), in Freidel, *Union Pamphlets*, 1: 299–300, 305, 313–14; [James Russell Lowell,] "The President's Policy," *North American Review*, 98 (January 1864): 260, and "The Rebellion: Its Causes and Consequences," ibid., 99 (July 1864): 267–68.

8. Walt Whitman, *Memoranda during the War* (Camden, N.J., 1875), p. 65, quoted in Rust, *Glory and Pathos*, pp. 112–13.

9. [Garrison,] *William Lloyd Garrison*, 4: 31, 167–68.

10. Maury, "Captain Maury's Letter on American Affairs" (Baltimore, 1861), reprinted in Freidel, *Union Pamphlets*, 1: 183.

11. C. Vann Woodward, ed., *Mary Chesnut's Civil War* (New Haven: Yale University Press, 1981), p. 109.

12. Catherine Ann Edmondston, *"Journal of a Secesh Lady": The Diary of Catherine Ann Devereux Edmondston, 1860–1866*, ed. Beth G. Crabtree and James W. Patton (Raleigh: North Carolina Division of Archives and History, 1979), pp. 180–81, 473, 716 and passim.

13. Avery Craven, *Edmund Ruffin, Southerner: A Study in Secession* (New York: D. Appleton, 1932), p. 259.

14. Howell Cobb (Macon, Ga.) to Brevet Major-General J. H. Wilson, June 14, 1865, in Andrew Johnson Papers, Library of Congress.

15. Stevens, speech in Lancaster, Pa., September 7, 1865, and Phillips, speech at Cooper Institute, New York, N.Y., October 25, 1866, both quoted in Howard K. Beale, *The Critical Year: A Study of Andrew Johnson and Reconstruction* (New York: Harcourt, Brace, 1930), pp. 149, 275–76; *The Complete Poetical Works of James Russell Lowell*, ed. Horace E. Scudder (Boston: Houghton Mifflin, 1925), p. 280.

16. Lancaster speech, September 7, 1865, quoted in Richard N. Current, *Old Thad Stevens: A Story of Ambition* (Madison: University of Wisconsin Press, 1942), p. 215.

17. Sumner, Senate speech of May 16, 1862, *Congressional Globe*, 37th Cong., 2nd sess., p. 2196.

18. Edward Atkinson, "The Future Supply of Cotton," *North American Review* 98 (April 1864): 485, 495–97.

19. Charles P. Kirkland, "The Mode of Restoration of the Rebel States to the Union," *The Merchants' Magazine and Commercial Review* 53 (July 1865): 30.

20. "Dedication of the Soldiers' Monument in Concord," April 19, 1867, in *The Complete Works of Ralph Waldo Emerson*, 12 vols. (Boston: Houghton Mifflin, 1911), 9: 355.

21. John A. Gillis (Victoria, Tex.) to Sister Hattie, November 21, 1855, in John Sherman Papers, Library of Congress.

22. William T. Sherman (St. Louis) to Willard Warner, January 16, 1866, in Warner Papers, Tennessee State Department of Archives, Nashville (microfilm in University of Alabama Library).

23. Whitelaw Reid, *After the War: A Southern Tour, May 1, 1865, to May 1, 1866* (Cincinnati and New York: Moore, Wilstach & Baldwin, 1866), pp. 240, 454–55, 560, 578–80; John T. Trowbridge, *The South:*

. . . *A Journey through the Desolated States* (Hartford, Conn.: L. Stebbins, 1866), p. 411; Sidney Andrews, *The South since the War* (Boston: Ticknor and Fields, 1866), pp. 1–5; *Harper's Weekly* 10 (October 6, 1866): 631.

24. Edward A. Pollard, *The Lost Cause: A New Southern History of the War of the Confederates* (New York: E. B. Treat, 1866), pp. 750–51; *Christian Index*, March 1866, and *Southern Review* [1867?], quoted in Charles R. Wilson, *Baptized in Blood: The Religion of the Lost Cause, 1865–1920* (Athens: University of Georgia Press, 1980), pp. 7, 84.

25. Jack P. Maddex, Jr., *The Reconstruction of Edward A. Pollard: A Rebel's Conversion to Postbellum Unionism* (Chapel Hill: University of North Carolina Press, 1974), pp. 72–73; *De Bow's Review* and *Putnam's Magazine*, quoted in Paul M. Gaston, *The New South Creed: A Study in Southern Mythmaking* (New York: Alfred A. Knopf, 1970), pp. 23, 33.

26. Trowbridge, *The South*, pp. 401–3; Philip H. Sheridan (New Orleans) to Henry Wilson, June 29, 1866, in Henry Wilson Papers, Library of Congress; David Macrae, *The Americans at Home* (1872; reprint ed., New York: E. P. Dutton, 1952), pp. 289–90.

27. Andrews, *The South since the War*, pp. 383–85, 397–98; Trowbridge, *The South*, p. 568; John R. Dennett, *The South As It Is, 1865–1866* (New York: Viking Press, 1965), pp. 306–10.

28. Letter from General A. L. Chatlain (Memphis), February 17, 1866, in *Chicago Tribune*, February 23, 1866; *Philadelphia Press*, November 15, 1867, quoted in *Littell's Living Age* 95 (December 1867): 679–81.

29. J. W. Sprague (Little Rock) to John Sherman, April 4, 1866, in Sherman Papers; Andrews, *The South since the War*, p. 320; *Philadelphia Press*, November 15, 1867, quoted in *Littell's Living Age* 95 (December 1867): 679–81.

30. "Special Correspondence, from M. H. P.," Charleston, S.C., August 23, 1867, in *Chicago Tribune*, August 28, 1867; Jacqueline Jones, *Soldiers of Light and Love: Northern Teachers and Georgia Blacks, 1865–1873* (Chapel Hill: University of North Carolina Press, 1980), pp. 5–9, 143–44, 154–61.

31. E. T. Herrick (New Orleans) to John Sherman, February 21, 1866, and Willard Warner (Prattville, Ala.) to William T. Sherman, April 22, 1866, both in John Sherman Papers; L. A. Sheldon (New Orleans) to James A. Garfield, January 17, 1866, in James A. Garfield Papers, Library of Congress; "The Rehabilitation of the South,"

Merchants' Magazine and Commercial Review 54 (March 1866): 169–74; Robert K. Scott (Charleston, S.C.) to Dear Doctor, August 16, 1866, in Robert K. Scott Papers, Ohio Historical Society, Columbus.

32. J. Davis, Jr. (Macon, Ga.), to John Sherman, November 30, 1865, in Sherman Papers.

33. G. F. Granger (Wilmington, N.C.) to Thaddeus Stevens, January 11, 1866, Thaddeus Stevens Papers, Library of Congress; Albion W. Tourgée, "Notes of a Speech in Pennsylvania, Fall of 1866," in Albion W. Tourgée Papers, Chautauqua County Historical Society, Westfield, N.Y. (microfilm in library of University of North Carolina at Greensboro).

34. See Jack B. Scroggs, "Carpetbagger Constitutional Reform in the South Atlantic States, 1867–1868," *Journal of Southern History* 27 (November 1961): 475–93; and Richard L. Hume, "The 'Black and Tan' Constitutional Conventions of 1867–1869 in Ten Former Confederate States: A Study of Their Membership" (Ph.D. dissertation, University of Washington, Seattle, 1969), pp. 656, 682–84.

35. Albion W. Tourgée, "Sarcastic Resolution on Radicals" and draft of speech on suffrage [1868], in Tourgée Papers; Powell Clayton, *The Aftermath of the Civil War in Arkansas* (New York: Neale Publishing, 1915), pp. 38–49; Warner, Senate remarks, January 26, 1870, *Congressional Globe*, 41st Cong., 2nd sess., pp. 788–89.

36. Russell H. Conwell, *Magnolia Journey: A Union Veteran Revisits the Former Confederate States*, ed. Joseph C. Carter (University, Ala.: University of Alabama Press, 1974), pp. 164–66; Robert Somers, *The Southern States since the War, 1870–71* (1871; reprint ed., University, Ala.: University of Alabama Press, 1971), pp. 93–98; Edward King, *The Great South* (Hartford, Conn.: American Publishing, 1875), 2: 283, 382, 385, 401, 420–21.

37. Holden, resolutions of the United Loyalists of America, January 31, 1868, in Raleigh *North Carolina Standard*, February 4, 1868; Vance, letter (Charlotte) declining the Conservative nomination for governor, March 6, 1868, in *Greensboro Times*, March 12, 1868; J. D. Hopkins (Newberry, S.C.) to Thaddeus Stevens, May 28, 1868, in Stevens Papers.

38. See Richard N. Current, "Carpetbaggers Reconsidered," in *A Festschrift for Frederick B. Artz*, ed. David M. Pinkney and Theodore Ropp (Durham, N.C.: Duke University Press, 1964), pp. 139–57.

39. Benjamin F. Perry to Robert K. Scott, March 13, 1871, in F. A. Porcher, "The Last Chapter in Reconstruction in South Carolina," *Southern Historical Society Papers* 12 (April 1884): 175–77; Charles

Nordhoff, *The Cotton States in the Spring and Summer of 1875* (1876; reprint ed., New York: Burt Franklin, n.d.), p. 81; "From Our Own Correspondent," Raleigh, N.C., July 16, 1872, *Chicago Tribune*, July 24, 1872.

40. Adelbert Ames to W. T. Sherman, August 17, 1869, quoted in William C. Harris, *The Day of the Carpetbagger: Republican Reconstruction in Mississippi* (Baton Rouge: Louisiana State University Press, 1979), pp. 57–58; Ames, Senate speech, April 11, 1871, *Congressional Globe*, 42nd Cong., 1st sess., pp. 569–71; Ames (New Orleans) to Mrs. Ames, August 7, 1874, in Blanche Butler Ames, ed., *Chronicles from the Nineteenth Century: Family Letters of Blanche Butler and Adelbert Ames*, 2 vols. (Clinton, Mass.: Colonial Press, 1957), 1: 702.

41. James Redpath, interview with Daniel H. Chamberlain, December 22–23, 1876, in *Chicago Tribune*, December 26, 28, 1876, and Chamberlain's July 4, 1877, address at Woodstock, Conn., both reprinted in Walter Allen, *Governor Chamberlain's Administration in South Carolina* (New York: G. P. Putnam's Sons, 1888), pp. 464–65, 507–20; "From Our Special Correspondent [H. C.]," New Orleans, April 26, 1877, in *New York Times*, April 30, 1877; Chamberlain, "Reconstruction and the Negro," *North American Review* 128 (February 1879): 173.

42. Interview with Tourgée in *New York Tribune*, September 3, 1879, quoted in Theodore L. Gross, *Albion W. Tourgée* (New York: Twayne, 1963), pp. 52–53; Tourgée, *A Fool's Errand* (New York: Fords, Howard, & Hulbert, 1879), pp. 340–41.

THREE
From New South to No South
1880s–1980s

1. Both quotations are from C. Vann Woodward, *Origins of the New South, 1877–1913* (Baton Rouge: Louisiana State University Press, 1951), p. 151.

2. Henry W. Grady, *The New South and Other Addresses*, ed. Edna Henry Lee Turpin (1904; reprint ed., New York: Haskell House, 1969), pp. 27–28, 33–34.

3. *New York Tribune*, March 11, 1881, quoted in Woodward, *Origins of the New South*, pp. 171–72; see also ibid., pp. 450–51; Dabney and the little girl quoted in Wilson, *Baptized in Blood*, pp. 24–25, 85–86.

4. Lady Duffus Hardy, *Down South* (London: Chapman and Hall, 1883), pp. 14–16.

5. Henry Martyn Field, *Blood Is Thicker Than Water: A Few Days among Our Southern Brethren* (New York: George Munro, 1886), pp. 19–20, 26, 107–8.

6. William D. Kelley, *The Old South and the New* (New York: G. P. Putnam's Sons, 1888), pp. 91, 121, 157, 161–62; *Philadelphia Times,* quoted in Woodward, *Origins of the New South,* p. 311.

7. *New York Tribune,* quoted in Woodward, *Origins of the New South,* p. 107; Hardy, *Down South,* pp. 118–19; Grady, *New South,* pp. 32, 96–98.

8. Warner to James B. Hill, September 19, 1882, in Warner Papers.

9. Albion W. Tourgée, *An Appeal to Caesar* (New York: Fords, Howard, & Hulbert, 1884), pp. 168–69.

10. Albert Bushnell Hart, *The Southern South* (New York: D. Appleton, 1910), pp. 48–50.

11. [E. L. Godkin,] "The White Side of the Southern Question," *The Nation* 31 (August 19, 1880): 126–27.

12. Grady, *New South,* p. 116.

13. Daniel H. Chamberlain, *Present Phase of Our So-Called Negro Problem* (1894), p. 24, quoted in Wilton B. Fowler, "A Carpetbagger's Conversion to White Supremacy," *North Carolina Historical Review* 43 (Summer 1966): 300–301.

14. Hart, *Southern South,* p. 74.

15. Albion W. Tourgée, "The South as a Field for Fiction," *The Forum* 6 (December 1888): 405; Joyce Appleby, "Reconciliation and the Northern Novelist, 1865–1880," *Civil War History* 10 (June 1964): 120.

16. Thomas Dixon, Jr., *The Leopard's Spots: A Romance of the White Man's Burden—1865–1900* (New York: Doubleday, Page, 1902), pp. 94–95, 435.

17. Albion W. Tourgée, *The Invisible Empire* (New York: Fords, Howard, & Hulbert, 1880), p. 395; Tourgée, *Appeal to Caesar,* pp. 68–71; Tourgée to Theodore Roosevelt, October 21, 1901, quoted in Roy F. Dibble, *Albion W. Tourgée* (New York: Lemcke & Buechner, 1921), pp. 126–27.

18. Oliver H. Orr, Jr., *Charles Brantley Aycock* (Chapel Hill: University of North Carolina Press, 1961), pp. 310–11; R. D. W. Connor and Clarence Poe, *The Life and Speeches of Charles Brantley Aycock* (New York: Doubleday, Page, 1912), pp. 130–31, 156, 280–81.

19. John M. Cooper, Jr., *Walter Hines Page: The Southerner as Amer-*

ican, 1855–1918 (Chapel Hill: University of North Carolina Press, 1977), pp. 80, 203; Walter Hines Page, *The Rebuilding of Old Commonwealths* (New York: Doubleday, Page, 1903), pp. 133–38, 151–53.

20. Hart, *Southern South*, pp. 2–3, 64–65.

21. H. L. Mencken, *The Bathtub Hoax and Other Blasts & Bravos from the Chicago Tribune*, ed. Robert McHugh (New York: Alfred A. Knopf, 1958), pp. 249, 251. See also George B. Tindall, *The Ethnic Southerners* (Baton Rouge: Louisiana State University Press, 1976), pp. 47–52.

22. Frank Tannenbaum, *Darker Phases of the South* (New York: G. P. Putnam's Sons, 1924), pp. 171–81.

23. William H. Skaggs, *The Southern Oligarchy: An Appeal in Behalf of the Silent Masses of Our Country against the Despotic Rule of the Few* (New York: Devin-Adair, 1924), pp. 421–23, 436. Skaggs, a former Populist, had served three terms as mayor of Talladega, Ala.

24. William J. Robertson, *The Changing South* (New York: Boni and Liveright, 1927), pp. 1–2, 50–51, 222–23.

25. Twelve Southerners, *I'll Take My Stand: The South and the Agrarian Tradition* (New York: Harper & Bros., 1930), pp. 63, 120–21, 336–37, 342. In addition to Owsley, Fletcher, and Young, the contributors to this book were John Crowe Ransom, Donald Davidson, Lyle H. Lanier, Allen Tate, Herman Clarence Nixon, Andrew Nelson Lytle, Robert Penn Warren, John Donald Wade, and Henry Blue Kline.

26. Mencken, *Bathtub Hoax*, pp. 251–54. See also Tindall, *Ethnic Southerners*, pp. 92–93, 111.

27. Howard W. Odum, *Southern Regions of the United States* (Chapel Hill: University of North Carolina Press, 1936), pp. 5, 55, 463, 525, 533, 543. This book was published "For the Southern Regional Committee of the Social Science Research Council." See also Howard W. Odum, *An American Epoch: Southern Portraiture in the National Picture* (New York: Henry Holt, 1930), pp. 68–86 ("The North Judges the South") and 87–101 ("The South Judges the North"). On the Agrarians and the Regionalists, see Michael O'Brien, *The Idea of the American South, 1920–1941* (Baltimore: Johns Hopkins University Press, 1979).

28. Quotations from Tindall, *Ethnic Southerners*, pp. 210–13.

29. National Emergency Council, *Report on Economic Conditions of the South* (Washington: Government Printing Office, 1938), pp. 1–2, 23, 34, 49, 59–60.

30. Cash, *The Mind of the South*, pp. 113–17, 145, 321–25 and passim.

31. On demographic changes, see Allan P. Sindler, ed., *Change in*

the Contemporary South (Durham, N.C.: Duke University Press, 1963), pp. 30–31, 113; Dudley J. Poston, Jr., and Robert H. Weller, eds., *The Population of the South: Structure and Change in Social Demographic Context* (Austin: University of Texas Press, 1981), pp. 13, 17–18, 123–26; Tindall, *Ethnic Southerners*, p. 230.

32. C. Vann Woodward, "The Search for Southern Identity," *Virginia Quarterly Review* (1958), reprinted in Woodward, *The Burden of Southern History* (Baton Rouge: Louisiana State University Press, 1960), pp. 7–8, 15–16, 23–24. Quotation of Woodward in 1972 is from John Egerton, *The Americanization of Dixie: The Southernization of America* (New York: Harper's Magazine Press, 1974), p. 13. There is an unconscious pun with unintended significance in Woodward's statement that the "bulldozer" would leave a deeper mark on the South than the carpetbagger had left. In the carpetbagger's usage of the 1870s, a "bulldozer" was a Democrat or a Conservative who used intimidation and force against the Republicans. That kind of "bulldozer" did indeed leave a deeper mark than the carpetbagger left.

33. Louis D. Rubin, Jr., ed., *The Lasting South: Fourteen Southerners Look at Their Home* (Chicago: Henry Regnery, 1957), pp. 51, 65, 126–27. Rubin himself, a Charleston native and in 1957 a professor of English at Hollins College, was pessimistic: "What has been distinctive and Southern about the South threatens to disappear, and the South threatens to become a thriving but undistinguished replica of the North and West, dependent upon the national industrial economy as never before" (pp. 13–14).

34. Sheldon Hackney, "Southern Violence," *American Historical Review* 74 (February 1969): 924–25. Hackney concludes: "From the southern past arise the symbiosis of profuse hospitality and intense hostility toward strangers and the paradox that the southern heritage is at the same time one of grace and violence" (p. 925).

35. Charles G. Sellers, introduction, and Thomas P. Govan, "Was the Old South Different," first published in *Journal of Southern History* (1955), both in Sellers, ed., *The Southerner as American*, pp. v, 38–39. The nine Southern historians, authors of these Sellers-edited essays, take a very different position from that of the fourteen literary scholars of the Rubin-edited volume published three years earlier.

36. Howard Zinn, *The Southern Mystique* (New York: Alfred A. Knopf, 1964), pp. 3, 217–18, 262; Frank E. Smith, *Look Away from Dixie* (Baton Rouge: Louisiana State University Press, 1965), p. 3; Pat Watters, *The South and the Nation* (New York: Pantheon Books, 1969), pp. ix-x.

37. Joseph B. Cumming, Jr., "Been Down Home So Long It Looks Like Up to Me: The Americanization of Dixie," *Esquire* 76 (August 1971): 85, 90; Egerton, *Americanization of Dixie*, p. xx; John Care, "An Interview with Walker Percy," *Georgia Review* 25 (Fall 1971): 319–20.

38. Lewis M. Killian, *White Southerners* (New York: Random House, 1970), pp. 88–89, 98–99, 113–15, 122–23.

39. John Shelton Reed, *The Enduring South: Subcultural Persistence in Mass Society* (1972; reprint ed., Chapel Hill: University of North Carolina Press, 1975), pp. 4, 10–11, 90. Reed reports (pp. 26–31) the results of a questionnaire given to 47 white Southern college students in 1970. They were asked to select from a list of 84 traits those that were most typical of white Southerners, white Northerners, and Americans. According to the students' responses, the most typical Northern and American traits were essentially the same, but the most typical Southern ones were different.

40. Tindall, *Ethnic Southerners*, pp. ix–xi.

41. Paul M. Gaston, "Sutpen's Door: The South since the *Brown* Decision," in Ernest M. Lander, Jr., and Richard J. Calhoun, eds., *Two Decades of Change: The South since the Supreme Court Desegregation Decision* (Columbia: University of South Carolina Press, 1975), pp. 101–2. This book contains papers presented at a Clemson University symposium, September 28–29, 1973.

42. *Milwaukee Journal*, June 7, 1981, "Accent," p. 7; *Greensboro Daily News*, September 28, 1981, sec. B, p. 1.

Assertions of the everlasting uniqueness of the South keep coming; the end is not in sight. In "The Ever-Vanishing South," his presidential address to the Southern Historical Association, November 12, 1981, Charles P. Roland insists that the South is not vanishing at all (*Journal of Southern History*, 47 [February 1982]: 3–20). In *Why the South Will Survive* (Athens: University of Georgia Press, 1981) fifteen Southern intellectuals offer a "manifesto of Southern pride" to mark the fiftieth anniversary of *I'll Take My Stand*.

Bibliography

THE FOLLOWING LIST OF SOURCES FOR THESE LECTURES DOES not pretend to exhaust the subject. No doubt a great deal has been said and recorded on the idea of Northernizing the South that is not mentioned here. Certainly the literature on the South itself is vast, and much of it bears upon the present subject.

Some manuscript collections have been consulted, and specific references to them are given in the notes. These collections are the papers of James A. Garfield, Andrew Johnson, Justin S. Morrill, John Sherman, Thaddeus Stevens, and Henry Wilson, all in the Library of Congress, Washington; the Robert K. Scott Papers, Ohio Historical Society, Columbus; the Albion W. Tourgée Papers, Chautauqua County Historical Society, Westfield, N.Y. (microfilm in library of University of North Carolina at Greensboro); and the Willard Warner Papers, Tennessee State Department of Archives, Nashville (microfilm in University of Alabama Library).

Several newspapers and news magazines have been used, among them the *Chicago Tribune*, the *Greensboro Times*, *Harper's Weekly*, *Littell's Living Age*, the *New York Times*, and the *Raleigh Standard*. Quotations have also been taken from the *Annals of Congress* and the *Congressional Globe*. The main reliance, however, has been on books and articles, as follows.

Abbott, John S. C. *South and North; or, Impressions Received during a Trip to Cuba and the South*. New York: Abbot & Abbot, 1860.

Adams, John Quincy, *Memoirs of John Quincy Adams, Comprising Portions of His Diary from 1795 to 1848*. Ed. Charles Francis Adams. 12 vols. Philadelphia: J. B. Lippincott, 1874–77.

Allen, Walter, *Governor Chamberlain's Administration in South Carolina*. New York: G. P. Putnam's Sons, 1888.

Ames, Blanche Butler, ed. *Chronicles from the Nineteenth Century: Family Letters of Blanche Butler and Adelbert Ames*. 2 vols. Clinton, Mass.: Colonial Press, 1957.

Andrews, Sidney. *The South since the War.* Boston: Ticknor and Fields, 1866.

Appleby, Joyce. "Reconciliation and the Northern Novelist, 1865–1880." *Civil War History* 10 (June 1864): 117–29.

Atkinson, Edward. "The Future Supply of Cotton." *North American Review* 98 (April 1864): 477–97.

Beale, Howard K. *The Critical Year: A Study of Andrew Johnson and Reconstruction.* New York: Harcourt, Brace, 1930.

Berger, Max. *The British Traveller in America, 1836–1860.* New York: Columbia University Press, 1943.

Bettersworth, John K. *Confederate Mississippi: The People and Policies of a Cotton State in Wartime.* Baton Rouge: Louisiana State University Press, 1943.

Buckingham, James S. *America: Historical, Statistic, and Descriptive.* 3 vols. London: Fisher, Son & Co., 1841.

Care, John. "An Interview with Walker Percy." *Georgia Review* 25 (Fall 1971): 317–32.

Cash, Wilbur J. *The Mind of the South.* 1941; reprint ed., Garden City, N.Y.: Doubleday, 1954.

Chamberlain, Daniel H. "Reconstruction and the Negro." *North American Review* 128 (February 1879): 161–73.

Clayton, Powell. *The Aftermath of the Civil War in Arkansas.* New York: Neale Publishing, 1915.

Connor, R. D. W., and Clarence Poe. *The Life and Speeches of Charles Brantley Aycock.* Garden City, N.Y.: Doubleday, Page, 1912.

Conwell, Russell H. *Magnolia Journey: A Union Veteran Revisits the Former Confederate States.* Ed. Joseph C. Carter. University, Ala.: University of Alabama Press, 1974.

Cooper, John M., Jr. *Walter Hines Page: The Southerner as American, 1855–1918.* Chapel Hill: University of North Carolina Press, 1977.

Craven, Avery. *Edmund Ruffin, Southerner: A Study in Secession.* New York: D. Appleton, 1932.

Cumming, Joseph B., Jr. "Been Down Home So Long It Looks Like Up to Me: The Americanization of Dixie." *Esquire* 76 (August 1971): 84–85 ff.

Current, Richard N. "Carpetbaggers Reconsidered." Pp. 139–157 in *A Festschrift for Frederick B. Artz,* ed. Theodore Ropp and David M. Pinkney. Durham, N.C.: Duke University Press, 1964.

———. *Old Thad Stevens: A Story of Ambition.* Madison: University of Wisconsin Press, 1942.

De Bow, J[ames]. D. B., ed. *The Industrial Resources, Statistics, Etc., of the United States and More Particularly of the Southern and Western States.* 1852; reprint. ed., New York: Augustus M. Kelley, 1966.

————. "The Non-Slaveholders of the South: Their Interest in the Present Sectional Controversy Identical with That of the Slaveholders." *De Bow's Review* 30 (January 1861): 67–77.

Dennett, John R. *The South As It Is, 1865–1866.* New York: Viking Press, 1965.

Dibble, Roy F. *Albion W. Tourgée.* New York: Lemcke & Buechner, 1921.

Dickey, Dallas C. *Seargent S. Prentiss: Whig Orator of the Old South.* Baton Rouge: Louisiana State University Press, 1945.

Dixon, Thomas, Jr. *The Leopard's Spots: A Romance of the White Man's Burden—1865–1900.* New York: Doubleday, Page, 1902.

Edmondston, Catherine Ann. *"Journal of a Secesh Lady": The Diary of Catherine Ann Devereux Edmondston, 1860–1866.* Ed. Beth G. Crabtree and James W. Patton. Raleigh: North Carolina Division of Archives and History, 1979.

Egerton, John. *The Americanization of Dixie: The Southernization of America.* New York: Harper's Magazine Press, 1974.

Emerson, Ralph Waldo. *The Complete Works of Ralph Waldo Emerson* 12 vols. Boston: Houghton Mifflin, 1911.

Field, Henry Martyn. *Blood Is Thicker Than Water: A Few Days among Our Southern Brethren.* New York: George Munro, 1886.

Fitzhugh, George. *Sociology for the South, or the Failure of Free Society.* 1854; reprint ed., New York: Burt Franklin, 1965.

Floan, Howard R. *The South in Northern Eyes, 1831–1861.* Austin: University of Texas Press, 1958.

Foner, Eric, *Free Soil, Free Labor, Free Men: The Ideology of the Republican Party before the Civil War.* New York: Oxford University Press, 1970.

Fowler, Wilton B. "A Carpetbagger's Conversion to White Supremacy." *North Carolina Historical Review* 43 (Summer 1966): 286–304.

Franklin, John Hope. *A Southern Odyssey: Travelers in the Antebellum North.* Baton Rouge: Louisiana State University Press, 1976.

Freidel, Frank, ed. *Union Pamphlets of the Civil War, 1861–1865.* 2 vols. Cambridge: Harvard University Press, 1967.

[Garrison, Wendell Phillips.] *William Lloyd Garrison, 1805–1879: The Story of His Life Told by His Children.* 4 vols. New York: Century, 1889.

Gaston, Paul M. *The New South Creed: A Study in Southern Mythmaking.* New York: Alfred A. Knopf, 1970.

[Godkin, E. L.] "The White Side of the Southern Question." *The Nation* 31 (August 19, 1880): 126–27.

Grady, Henry W. *The New South and Other Addresses.* Ed. Edna Henry Lee Turpin. 1904; reprint ed., New York: Haskell House, 1969.

Green, Fletcher M. *The Role of the Yankee in the Old South.* Athens: University of Georgia Press, 1972.

Gross, Theodore L. *Albion W. Tourgée.* New York: Twayne, 1963.

Hackney, Sheldon. "Southern Violence." *American Historical Review* 74 (February 1969): 906–25.

Hamilton, Thomas. *Men and Manners in America.* 1833; reprint ed., New York: Russell & Russell, 1968.

Hardy, Lady Duffus. *Down South.* London: Chapman and Hall, 1883.

Harris, William C. *The Day of the Carpetbagger: Republican Reconstruction in Mississippi.* Baton Rouge: Louisiana State University Press, 1979.

Hart, Albert Bushnell. *The Southern South.* New York: D. Appleton, 1910.

Helper, Hinton Rowan. *The Impending Crisis of the South: How to Meet It.* 1857; reprint ed., New York: A. B. Burdick, 1860.

Holmes, Oliver Wendell. *The Works of Oliver Wendell Holmes.* 13 vols. Boston: Houghton Mifflin, 1892.

Hume, Richard L. "The 'Black and Tan' Constitutional Conventions of 1867–1869 in Ten Former Confederate States: A Study of Their Membership." Ph.D. dissertation, University of Washington, Seattle, 1969.

Hundley, Daniel R. *Social Relations in Our Southern States.* 1860; reprint ed., Baton Rouge; Louisiana State University Press, 1979.

Jefferson, Thomas. *Notes on the State of Virginia.* 1787; reprint ed. Chapel Hill: University of North Carolina Press, 1955.

———. *The Papers of Thomas Jefferson.* Vol. 8. Ed. Julian P. Boyd. Princeton: Princeton University Press, 1953.

Jones, Jacqueline. *Soldiers of Light and Love: Northern Teachers and Georgia Blacks, 1865–1873.* Chapel Hill: University of North Carolina Press, 1980.

Kelley, William D. *The Old South and the New.* New York: G. P. Putnam's Sons, 1888.

Killian, Lewis M. *White Southerners.* New York: Random House, 1970.

King, Edward. *The Great South.* Hartford, Conn.: American Publishing, 1875.

Kirkland, Charles P. "The Mode of Restoration of the Rebel States to the Union." *The Merchants' Magazine and Commercial Review* 53 (July 1865): 19–30.

Lander, Ernest M., Jr., and Richard J. Calhoun, eds. *Two Decades of Change: The South since the Supreme Court Desegregation Decision.* Columbia: University of South Carolina Press, 1975.

Lowell, James Russell. *The Complete Poetical Works of James Russell Lowell.* Ed. Horace E. Scudder. Boston: Houghton Mifflin, 1925.

[————.] "The President's Policy." *North American Review* 98 (January 1864): 234–60.

[————.] "The Rebellion: Its Causes and Consequences." *North American Review* 99 (July 1864): 246–68.

McCardell, John. *The Idea of a Southern Nation: Southern Nationalists and Southern Nationalism, 1830–1860.* New York: W. W. Norton, 1979.

Maclay, William. *Journal of William Maclay, United States Senator from Pennsylvania, 1789–1791.* Ed. Edgar S. Maclay. New York: D. Appleton, 1890.

Macrae, David. *The Americans at Home.* 1872; reprint ed., New York: E. P. Dutton, 1952.

Maddex, Jack P., Jr. *The Reconstruction of Edward A. Pollard: A Rebel's Conversion to Postbellum Unionism.* Chapel Hill: University of North Carolina Press, 1974.

Madison, James. *Journal of the Federal Convention Kept by James Madison.* 1840; reprint ed., Chicago: Albert, Scott, 1893.

Mencken, H[enry]. L[ewis]. *The Bathtub Hoax and Other Blasts & Bravos from the Chicago Tribune.* Ed. Robert McHugh. New York: Alfred A. Knopf, 1958.

Mesick, Jane Louise. *The English Traveller in America, 1785–1835.* 1922; reprint ed., Westport, Conn.: Greenwood Press, 1970.

Moore, Glover. *The Missouri Controversy, 1819–1821.* 1953; reprint ed., Lexington: University of Kentucky Press, 1966.

Moore, J. Quitman. "National Characteristics—the Issues of the Day." *De Bow's Review* 30 (January 1861): 42–52.

National Emergency Council. *Report on Economic Conditions of the South.* Washington: Government Printing Office, 1938.

Nordhoff, Charles. *The Cotton States in the Spring and Summer of 1875.* 1876; reprint ed., New York: Burt Franklin, n.d.

O'Brien, Michael. *The Idea of the American South, 1920–1941.* Baltimore: Johns Hopkins University Press, 1979.

Odum, Howard W. *An American Epoch: Southern Portraiture in the National Picture.* New York: Henry Holt, 1930.

————. *Southern Regions of the United States.* Chapel Hill: University of North Carolina Press, 1936.

Olmsted, Frederick Law. *The Cotton Kingdom: A Traveller's Observations on Cotton and Slavery in the American Slave States, Based upon Three Former Volumes of Journeys and Investigations by the Same Author.* 1861; reprint ed., New York: Alfred A. Knopf, 1953.

Orr, Oliver H., Jr. *Charles Brantley Aycock.* Chapel Hill: University of North Carolina Press, 1961.

Page, Walter Hines. *The Rebuilding of Old Commonwealths.* New York: Doubleday, Page, 1903.

Perkins, Howard C., ed. *Northern Editorials on Secession.* 2 vols. New York: D. Appleton-Century, 1942.

Pollard, Edward A. *The Lost Cause: A New Southern History of the War of the Confederates.* New York: E. B. Treat, 1866.

Porcher, F. A. "The Last Chapter in Reconstruction in South Carolina." *Southern Historical Society Papers* 12 (April 1884): 173–81.

Poston, Dudley J., Jr., and Robert H. Weller, eds. *The Population of the South: Structure and Change in Social Demographic Context.* Austin: University of Texas Press, 1981.

[Prentiss, George Lewis, ed.] *A Memoir of S. S. Prentiss.* 2 vols. 1855; reprint ed., New York: Charles Scribner's Sons, 1879.

Pulszky, Francis and Theresa. *White Red Black: Sketches of Society in the United States during the Visit of Their Guest* [Louis Kossuth]. 1853; reprint ed., New York: Negro Universities Press, 1968.

Raumer, Frederick von. *America and the American People.* Trans. William W. Turner. New York: J. & H. G. Langley, 1846.

Reed, John Shelton. *The Enduring South: Subcultural Persistence in Mass Society.* 1972; reprint ed., Chapel Hill: University of North Carolina Press, 1975.

Reid, Whitelaw. *After the War: A Southern Tour, May 1, 1865, to May 1, 1866.* Cincinnati and New York: Wilstach & Baldwin, 1866.

Robertson, William J. *The Changing South.* New York: Boni and Liveright, 1927.

Rubin, Louis D., ed. *The Lasting South: Fourteen Southerners Look at Their Home.* Chicago: Henry Regnery, 1957.

Rust, Richard D., ed. *Glory and Pathos: Responses of Nineteenth-Century American Authors to the Civil War.* Boston: Holbrook Press, 1970.

Scroggs, Jack B. "Carpetbagger Constitutional Reform in the South Atlantic States, 1867–1868." *Journal of Southern History* 27 (November 1961): 475–93.

Sellers, Charles G., ed. *The Southerner as American.* Chapel Hill: University of North Carolina Press, 1960.

Sindler, Allan P., ed. *Change in the Contemporary South.* Durham, N.C.: Duke University Press, 1963.

Skaggs, William H. *The Southern Oligarchy: An Appeal in Behalf of the*

Silent Masses of Our Country against the Despotic Rule of the Few. New York: Devin-Adair, 1924.

Smith, Frank E. *Look Away from Dixie.* Baton Rouge: Louisiana State University Press, 1965.

Somers, Robert. *The Southern States since the War, 1870–71.* 1871; reprint ed., University: University of Alabama Press, 1971.

Stirling, James. *Letters from the Slave States.* London: John W. Parker and Son, 1857.

Tannenbaum, Frank. *Darker Phases of the South.* New York: G. P. Putnam's Sons, 1924.

Taylor, William R. *Cavalier and Yankee: The Old South and American National Character.* 1961; reprint ed., Garden City, N.Y.: Doubleday, 1963.

Tindall, George B. *The Ethnic Southerners.* Baton Rouge: Louisiana State University Press, 1976.

Tocqueville, Alexis de. *Democracy in America.* Trans. Henry Reeve. 1835–40; reprint ed., New York: D. Appleton, 1904.

Tourgée, Albion W. *An Appeal to Caesar.* New York: Fords, Howard, & Hulbert, 1884.

———. *A Fool's Errand.* New York: Fords, Howard, & Hulbert, 1879.

———. *The Invisible Empire.* New York: Fords, Howard, & Hulbert, 1880.

———. "The South as a Field for Fiction." *The Forum* 6 (December 1888): 404–13.

Trowbridge, John T. *The South: . . . A Journey through the Desolated States.* Hartford, Conn.: L. Stebbins, 1866.

Twelve Southerners. *I'll Take My Stand: The South and the Agrarian Tradition.* New York: Harper & Bros., 1930.

Watters, Pat. *The South and the Nation.* New York: Pantheon Books, 1969.

Whipple, Henry B. *Bishop Whipple's Southern Diary, 1843–1844.* Ed. L. B. Shippee. Minneapolis: University of Minnesota Press, 1937.

Wilson, Charles R. *Baptized in Blood: The Religion of the Lost Cause, 1865–1920.* Athens: University of Georgia Press, 1980.

Woodward, C. Vann. *The Burden of Southern History.* Baton Rouge: Louisiana State University Press, 1960.

———. *Origins of the New South, 1877–1913.* Baton Rouge: Louisiana State University Press, 1951.

———, ed. *Mary Chesnut's Civil War.* New Haven: Yale University Press, 1981.

Zinn, Howard. *The Southern Mystique.* New York: Alfred A. Knopf, 1964.

Index